Parisian Nights

12 designs by Marie Wallin, Martin Storey & Lisa Richardson using Kidsilk Haze, Fine Lace & Anchor Artiste Metallic

Parisian Nights

Over the last few seasons we have had many requests for eveningwear designs using our ever popular and beautiful Kidsilk Haze yarn. We are therefore very pleased to introduce our new 'Parisian Nights' collection to you.

This sophisticated and elegant collection with designs by Marie Wallin, Martin Storey and Lisa Richardson is a 'must have' for the party season.

Using Kidsilk Haze, our exquisite Fine Lace and the Anchor Artiste Metallic yarn, we have designed a collection which will definitely compliment your party and eveningwear wardrobe. Some of the pieces can be worn as daywear and then restyled to wear for a glamorous evening out.

Photographed at night in the romantic city of Paris, we hope that the amazing and dramatic imagery will inspire you to create your own piece of glamour for a 'Parisian Night' out.

Chenin

By Marie Wallin
Using Kidsilk Haze
Pattern page 47

Burgundy

By Lisa Richardson
Using Kidsilk Haze
Pattern page 32

Pinot

By Martin Storey
Using Kidsilk Haze &
Anchor Artiste Metallic
Pattern page 61

Muscadet
By Marie Wallin
Using Kidsilk Haze
& Anchor Artiste Metallic
Pattern page 53

Champagne

By Marie Wallin
Using Kidsilk Haze & Fine Lace
Pattern page 41

Sauvignon

By Martin Storey
Using Kidsilk Haze
Pattern page 63

Cabernet

By Lisa Richardson
Using Kidsilk Haze
& Anchor Artiste Metallic
Pattern page 35

Semillon

By Martin Storey
Using Kidsilk Haze
Pattern page 65

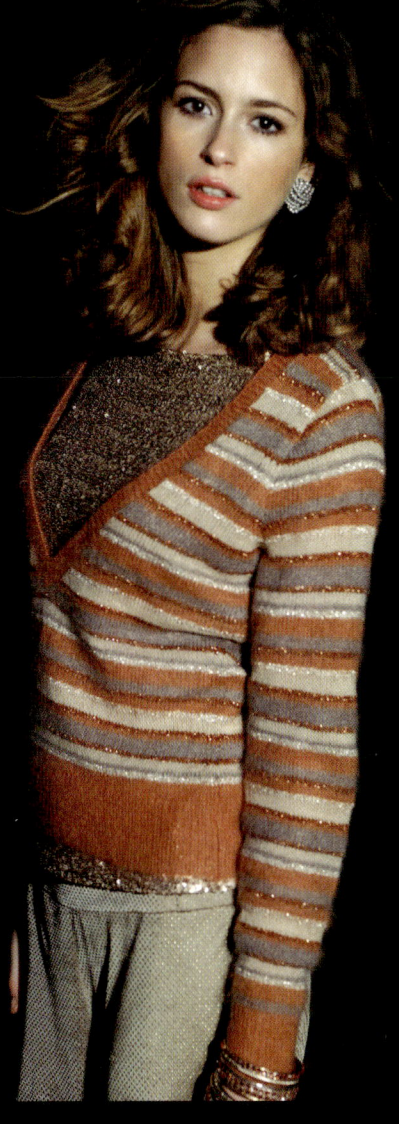

Viognier

By Lisa Richardson
Using Kidsilk Haze
& Anchor Artiste Metallic
Pattern page 67

Merlot

By Marie Wallin
Using Kidsilk Haze
& Anchor Artiste Metallic
Pattern page 51

Chardonnay
By Marie Wallin
Using Kidsilk Haze
Pattern page 43

Chablis

By Marie Wallin
Using Kidsilk Haze & Fine Lace
Pattern page 38

Yarn Information

Kidsilk Haze Z012000

Our ever popular Kidsilk Haze is a beautiful and versatile fine yarn made from a blend of super kid mohair and silk.

Mud 652	Fudge 658	Marmalade 596	Brick 649	Ember 644	Essence 663	Meadow 581	Jelly 597	Fern 629	Forest Green 651
Trance 582	Alhambra 666	Pearl 590	Grace 580	Shadow 653	Rosso 661	Blushes 583	Candy Girl 606	Blood 627	Liqueur 595
Dewberry 600	Hibiscus 665	Ultra 659	Cream 634	Steel 664	Ghost 642	Mist 636	Heavenly 592	Turkish Plum 660	Hurricane 632
Blackcurrant 641	Smoke 605	Anthracite 639	Wicked 599	Majestic 589	Splendour 579				

Fine Lace 9802140

This beautiful fine lace weight yarn is made in a blend of the softest baby suri alpaca and the finest merino wool. This gorgeous, luxurious yarn is perfect for creating delicate hand knitted and crochet lace

| Porcelaine 928 | Cameo 920 | Ochre 930 | Vamp 935 | Quaint 925 | Antique 921 | Gunmetal 929 | Noir 934 |

| Era 927 | Vintage 926 | Jewel 936 | Retro 923 | Cobweb 922 | Aged 933 | Patina 924 | Leaf 931 |

Anchor Artiste Metallic 4716400

300 | 301 | 318 | 319 | 320 | 321 | 322 | 328 | 330 | 332

313 | 303 | 304 | 312 | 308 | 310 | 306 | 311 | 302 | 314

Burgundy ★★★
By Lisa Richardson

Main Image Page 6

SIZES

S	M	L	XL	XXL	
To fit bust					
81-86	91-97	102-107	112-117	122-127	cm
32-34	36-38	40-42	44-46	48-50	in

YARN
Kidsilk Haze

3	4	4	4	5	x 25gm

(photographed in Liqueur 595)

NEEDLES
1 pair 3¼mm (no 10) (US 3) needles
1 pair 4mm (no 8) (US 6) needles
2 cable needles

BUTTONS - 2 x RW5019 from Bedecked. Please see information page for contact details.

TENSION
21 sts and 29 rows to 10 cm measured over patt using 4mm (US 6) needles.

SPECIAL ABBREVIATION
C6F = slip next st onto first cable needle and leave at front of work, slip next 4 sts onto 2nd cable needle and leave at back of work, K1, then K4 from 2nd cable needle, then K1 from first cable needle.

FRONT
Using 3¼mm (US 3) needles cast on 92 [102: 116: 128: 142] sts.
Work in g st for 4 rows, ending with RS facing for next row.
Change to 4mm (US 6) needles.
Work in patt as folls:
Row 1 (RS): P8 [6: 6: 5: 5], K1, K2tog, (yfwd) twice, sl 1, K1, psso, K1, *P1, K1, K2tog, (yfwd) twice, sl 1, K1, psso, K1, rep from * to last 8 [6: 6: 5: 5] sts, P8 [6: 6: 5: 5].
Row 2: K8 [6: 6: 5: 5], P2, (P1, P1 tbl) into double yfwd of previous row, P2, *K1, P2, (P1, P1 tbl) into double yfwd of previous row, P2, rep from * to last 8 [6: 6: 5: 5] sts, K8 [6: 6: 5: 5].
Row 3: P8 [6: 6: 5: 5], K1, yfwd, K2tog, sl 1, K1, psso, yfwd, K1, *P1, K1, yfwd, K2tog, sl 1, K1, psso, yfwd, K1, rep from * to last 8 [6: 6: 5: 5] sts, P8 [6: 6: 5: 5].
Row 4: K8 [6: 6: 5: 5], P6, *K1, P6, rep from * to last 8 [6: 6: 5: 5] sts, K8 [6: 6: 5: 5].
Rows 5 and 6: As rows 1 and 2.
Row 7: P8 [6: 6: 5: 5], C6F, *P1, K1, yfwd, K2tog, sl 1, K1, psso, yfwd, K1, P1, C6F, rep from * to last 8 [6: 6: 5: 5] sts, P8 [6: 6: 5: 5].
Row 8: As row 4.
Rows 9 to 12: As rows 1 to 4.
Rows 13 and 14: As rows 1 and 2.
Row 15: P8 [6: 6: 5: 5], K1, yfwd, K2tog, sl 1, K1, psso, yfwd, K1, *P1, C6F, P1, K1, yfwd, K2tog, sl 1, K1, psso, yfwd, K1, rep from * to last 8 [6: 6: 5: 5] sts, P8 [6: 6: 5: 5].
Row 16: As row 4.
These 16 rows form patt.
Cont in patt, dec 1 st at each end of next [next: 3rd: 3rd: 5th] and 2 foll 8th rows. 86 [96: 110: 122: 136] sts.
Work 17 [19: 19: 21: 21] rows, ending with RS facing for next row.
Inc 1 st at each end of next and 2 foll 12th rows.
92 [102: 116: 128: 142] sts.
Work 19 [21: 21: 23: 23] rows, ending with RS facing for next row.
(Front should meas approx 34 [35: 36: 37: 38] cm.)

Shape armholes
Keeping patt correct, cast off 4 [5: 6: 7: 8] sts at beg of next 2 rows.
84 [92: 104: 114: 126] sts.
Dec 1 st at each end of next 3 [5: 5: 7: 7] rows, then on foll 3 [3: 6: 6: 8] alt rows. 72 [76: 82: 88: 96] sts.
Cont straight until armhole meas 15 [16: 16: 17: 17] cm, ending with RS facing for next row.

Shape front neck
Next row (RS): Patt 19 [21: 24: 27: 31] sts and turn, leaving rem sts on a holder.
Work each side of neck separately.
Dec 1 st at neck edge of next 8 rows, then on foll 1 [1: 2: 2: 3] alt rows.
10 [12: 14: 17: 20] sts.
Cont straight until armhole meas 20 [21: 22: 23: 24] cm, ending with

RS facing for next row.
Shape shoulder
Cast off 3 [4: 5: 6: 7] sts at beg of next and foll alt row.
Work 1 row.
Cast off rem 4 [4: 4: 5: 6] sts.
With RS facing, rejoin yarn to rem sts, cast off centre 34 sts, patt to end.
Complete to match first side, reversing shapings.

RIGHT BACK
Using 3¼mm (US 3) needles cast on 21 [19: 19: 18: 18] sts.
Work in g st for 4 rows, inc 1 st at end of 3rd of these rows and ending with RS facing for next row. 22 [20: 20: 19: 19] sts.
Change to 4mm (US 6) needles.
Work in patt as folls:
Row 1 (RS): P8 [6: 6: 5: 5], *K1, K2tog, (yfwd) twice, sl 1, K1, psso, K1*, P1, rep from * to * once more, inc in last st. 23 [21: 21: 20: 20] sts.
Row 2: P1, *K1, P2, (P1, P1 tbl) into double yfwd of previous row, P2, rep from * once more, K8 [6: 6: 5: 5].
Row 3: P8 [6: 6: 5: 5], (K1, yfwd, K2tog, sl 1, K1, psso, yfwd, K1, P1) twice, inc in last st. 24 [22: 22: 21: 21] sts.
Row 4: P2, (K1, P6) twice, K8 [6: 6: 5: 5].
Row 5: P8 [6: 6: 5: 5], *K1, K2tog, (yfwd) twice, sl 1, K1, psso, K1, P1, rep from * once more, K1, inc in last st. 25 [23: 23: 22: 22] sts.
Row 6: P3, *K1, P2, (P1, P1 tbl) into double yfwd of previous row, P2, rep from * once more, K8 [6: 6: 5: 5].
Row 7: P8 [6: 6: 5: 5], C6F, P1, K1, yfwd, K2tog, sl 1, K1, psso, yfwd, K1, P1, K2, inc in last st. 26 [24: 24: 23: 23] sts.
Row 8: P4, (K1, P6) twice, K8 [6: 6: 5: 5].
Row 9: P8 [6: 6: 5: 5], *K1, K2tog, (yfwd) twice, sl 1, K1, psso, K1, P1, rep from * once more, K1, K2tog, yfwd, inc in last st.
27 [25: 25: 24: 24] sts.
Row 10: P5, *K1, P2, (P1, P1 tbl) into double yfwd of previous row, P2, rep from * once more, K8 [6: 6: 5: 5].
Row 11: P8 [6: 6: 5: 5], (K1, yfwd, K2tog, sl 1, K1, psso, yfwd, K1, P1) twice, K1, yfwd, K2tog, K1, inc in last st. 28 [26: 26: 25: 25] sts.
Row 12: P6, (K1, P6) twice, K8 [6: 6: 5: 5].
Row 13: P8 [6: 6: 5: 5], *K1, K2tog, (yfwd) twice, sl 1, K1, psso, K1, P1, rep from * once more, (yfwd) twice, sl 1, K1, psso, inc in last st. 29 [27: 27: 26: 26] sts.
Row 14: *K1, P2, (P1, P1 tbl) into double yfwd of previous row, P2, rep from * twice more, K8 [6: 6: 5: 5].
Row 15: P8 [6: 6: 5: 5], K1, yfwd, K2tog, sl 1, K1, psso, yfwd, K1, P1, C6F, P1, K1, yfwd, K2tog, sl 1, K1, psso, yfwd, K1, inc in last st.
30 [28: 28: 27: 27] sts.
Row 16: P1, (K1, P6) 3 times, K8 [6: 6: 5: 5].
These 16 rows form patt and beg back opening edge shaping.
Cont in patt, dec 1 st at beg of next [next: 3rd: 3rd: 5th] and 2 foll 8th rows **and at same time** inc 1 st at back opening edge of next and foll 1 [8: 9: 9: 10] alt rows, then on 3 [0: 0: 0: 0] foll 4th rows, taking inc sts into patt. 32 [34: 35: 34: 35] sts.
Work 17 [19: 19: 21: 21] rows, inc 1 st at back opening edge of 2nd and foll 0 [3: 8: 9: 9] alt rows, then on 3 [2: 0: 0: 0] foll 4th rows and ending with RS facing for next row. 36 [40: 44: 44: 45] sts.

Inc 1 st at beg of next and 2 foll 12th rows **and at same time** inc 1 st at back opening edge of next and foll 0 [0: 4: 12: 12] alt rows, then on 6 [6: 4: 0: 0] foll 4th rows. 46 [50: 56: 60: 61] sts.
Work 19 [21: 21: 23: 23] rows, inc 1 st at back opening edge of 4th [4th: 4th: 2nd: 2nd] and foll 0 [0: 0: 1: 10] alt rows, then on 3 [4: 4: 4: 0] foll 4th rows and ending with RS facing for next row.
50 [55: 61: 66: 72] sts.
Shape armhole
Keeping patt correct, cast off 4 [5: 6: 7: 8] sts at beg and inc 1 [0: 0: 1: 1] st at end of next row. 47 [50: 55: 60: 65] sts.
Work 1 row.
Dec 1 st at armhole edge of next 3 [5: 5: 7: 7] rows, then on foll 3 [3: 6: 6: 8] alt rows **and at same time** inc 1 st at back opening edge of 3rd [next: next: 3rd: 3rd] and 1 [2: 4: 4: 5] foll 4th rows.
43 [45: 49: 52: 56] sts.
Inc 1 st at back opening edge of 2nd [2nd: 4th: 4th: 4th] and 7 [7: 6: 6: 6] foll 4th rows. 51 [53: 56: 59: 63] sts.
Cont straight until 5 rows less have been worked than on front to beg of shoulder shaping, ending with **WS** facing for next row.
Shape back neck
Keeping patt correct, cast off 35 [35: 36: 36: 37] sts at beg of next row, placing marker after 15th cast-off st. 16 [18: 20: 23: 26] sts.
Dec 1 st at neck edge of next 4 rows, ending with RS facing for next row. 12 [14: 16: 19: 22] sts.
Shape shoulder
Cast off 3 [4: 5: 6: 7] sts at beg of next and foll alt row **and at same time** dec 1 st at neck edge of next and foll alt row.
Work 1 row.
Cast off rem 4 [4: 4: 5: 6] sts.

LEFT BACK
Using 3¼mm (US 3) needles cast on 21 [19: 19: 18: 18] sts.
Work in g st for 4 rows, inc 1 st at beg of 3rd of these rows and ending with RS facing for next row. 22 [20: 20: 19: 19] sts.
Change to 4mm (US 6) needles.
Work in patt as folls:
Row 1 (RS): Inc in first st, K1, K2tog, (yfwd) twice, sl 1, K1, psso, K1, P1, K1, K2tog, (yfwd) twice, sl 1, K1, psso, K1, P8 [6: 6: 5: 5].
23 [21: 21: 20: 20] sts.
Row 2: K8 [6: 6: 5: 5], *P2, (P1, P1 tbl) into double yfwd of previous row, P2, K1, rep from * once more, P1.
Row 3: Inc in first st, (P1, K1, yfwd, K2tog, sl 1, K1, psso, yfwd, K1) twice, P8 [6: 6: 5: 5]. 24 [22: 22: 21: 21] sts.
Row 4: K8 [6: 6: 5: 5], (P6, K1) twice, P2.
Row 5: Inc in first st, K1, *P1, K1, K2tog, (yfwd) twice, sl 1, K1, psso, K1, rep from * once more, P8 [6: 6: 5: 5]. 25 [23: 23: 22: 22] sts.
Row 6: K8 [6: 6: 5: 5], *P2, (P1, P1 tbl) into double yfwd of previous row, P2, K1, rep from * once more, P3.
Row 7: Inc in first st, K2, P1, K1, yfwd, K2tog, sl 1, K1, psso, yfwd, K1, P1, C6F, P8 [6: 6: 5: 5]. 26 [24: 24: 23: 23] sts.
Row 8: K8 [6: 6: 5: 5], (P6, K1) twice, P4.
Row 9: Inc in first st, yfwd, sl 1, K1, psso, K1, *P1, K1, K2tog, (yfwd) twice, sl 1, K1, psso, K1, rep from * once more, P8 [6: 6: 5: 5].

27 [25: 25: 24: 24] sts.
Row 10: K8 [6: 6: 5: 5], *P2, (P1, P1 tbl) into double yfwd of previous row, P2, K1, rep from * once more, P5.
Row 11: Inc in first st, K1, sl 1, K1, psso, yfwd, K1, (P1, K1, yfwd, K2tog, sl 1, K1, psso, yfwd, K1) twice, P8 [6: 6: 5: 5]. 28 [26: 26: 25: 25] sts.
Row 12: K8 [6: 6: 5: 5], (P6, K1) twice, P6.
Row 13: Inc in first st, K2tog, (yfwd) twice, sl 1, K1, psso, K1, *P1, K1, K2tog, (yfwd) twice, sl 1, K1, psso, K1, rep from * once more, P8 [6: 6: 5: 5]. 29 [27: 27: 26: 26] sts.
Row 14: K8 [6: 6: 5: 5], *P2, (P1, P1 tbl) into double yfwd of previous row, P2, K1, rep from * twice more.
Row 15: Inc in first st, K1, yfwd, K2tog, sl 1, K1, psso, yfwd, K1, P1, C6F, P1, K1, yfwd, K2tog, sl 1, K1, psso, yfwd, K1, P8 [6: 6: 5: 5]. 30 [28: 28: 27: 27] sts.
Row 16: K8 [6: 6: 5: 5], (P6, K1) 3 times, P1.
These 16 rows form patt and beg back opening edge shaping.
Complete to match right back, reversing shapings.

SLEEVES
Using 3¼mm (US 3) needles cast on 40 [42: 44: 44: 46] sts.
Work in g st for 4 rows, ending with RS facing for next row.
Change to 4mm (US 6) needles.
Work in patt as folls:
Row 1 (RS): K2 [3: 1: 1: 2], (yfwd, sl 1, K1, psso, K1) 0 [0: 1: 1: 1] times, *P1, K1, K2tog, (yfwd) twice, sl 1, K1, psso, K1, rep from * to last 3 [4: 5: 5: 6] sts, P1, (K1, K2tog, yfwd) 0 [0: 1: 1: 1] times, K2 [3: 1: 1: 2].
Row 2: P2 [3: 4: 4: 5], K1, *P2, (P1, P1 tbl) into double yfwd of previous row, P2, K1, rep from * to last 2 [3: 4: 4: 5] sts, P2 [3: 4: 4: 5].
Row 3: K2 [3: 1: 1: 2], (sl 1, K1, psso, yfwd, K1) 0 [0: 1: 1: 1] times, *P1, K1, yfwd, K2tog, sl 1, K1, psso, K1, rep from * to last 3 [4: 5: 5: 6] sts, P1, (K1, yfwd, K2tog) 0 [0: 1: 1: 1] times, K2 [3: 1: 1: 2].
Row 4: P2 [3: 4: 4: 5], K1, *P6, K1, rep from * to last 2 [3: 4: 4: 5] sts, P2 [3: 4: 4: 5].
Row 5: Inc in first st, K1 [2: 0: 0: 1], (yfwd, sl 1, K1, psso, K1) 0 [0: 1: 1: 1] times, *P1, K1, K2tog, (yfwd) twice, sl 1, K1, psso, K1, rep from * to last 3 [4: 5: 5: 6] sts, P1, (K1, K2tog, yfwd) 0 [0: 1: 1: 1] times, K1 [2: 0: 0: 1], inc in last st. 42 [44: 46: 46: 48] sts.
Row 6: P3 [4: 5: 5: 6], K1, *P2, (P1, P1 tbl) into double yfwd of previous row, P2, K1, rep from * to last 3 [4: 5: 5: 6] sts, P3 [4: 5: 5: 6].
Row 7: K0 [1: 2: 2: 1], (yfwd, K2tog) 0 [0: 0: 0: 1] times, sl 1, K1, psso, yfwd, K1, *P1, C6F, P1, K1, yfwd, K2tog, sl 1, K1, psso, yfwd, K1, rep from * to last 11 [12: 13: 13: 14] sts, P1, C6F, P1, K1, yfwd, K2tog, (sl 1, K1, psso, yfwd) 0 [0: 0: 0: 1] times, K0 [1: 2: 2: 1].
Row 8: P3 [4: 5: 5: 6], K1, *P6, K1, rep from * to last 3 [4: 5: 5: 6] sts, P3 [4: 5: 5: 6].
Row 9: K3 [1: 2: 2: 1], (K2tog, yfwd) 0 [0: 0: 0: 1] times, (yfwd, sl 1, K1, psso, K1) 0 [1: 1: 1: 1] times, *P1, K1, K2tog, (yfwd) twice, sl 1, K1, psso, K1, rep from * to last 4 [5: 6: 6: 0] sts, P1 [1: 1: 1: 0], (K1, K2tog, yfwd) 0 [1: 1: 1: 0] times, K3 [1: 2: 2: 0].
Row 10: P3 [4: 5: 5: 0], K1 [1: 1: 1: 0], *P2, (P1, P1 tbl) into double yfwd of previous row, P2, K1, rep from * to last 3 [4: 5: 5: 6] sts, P3 [4: 5: 5: 2], (P1 and P1 tbl into double yfwd of previous row, P2) 0 [0: 0: 0: 1] times.
Row 11: (Inc in first st) 0 [1: 1: 1: 1] times, K0 [0: 1: 1: 0], (yfwd, K2tog) 0 [0: 0: 0: 1] times, sl 1, K1, psso, yfwd, K1, *P1, K1, yfwd, K2tog, sl 1, K1, psso, yfwd, K1, rep from * to last 4 [5: 6: 6: 7] sts, P1, K1, yfwd, K2tog, (sl 1, K1, psso, yfwd) 0 [0: 0: 0: 1] times, K0 [0: 1: 1: 0], (inc in last st) 0 [1: 1: 1: 1] times. 42 [46: 48: 48: 50] sts.
Row 12: P3 [5: 6: 6: 0], K1, *P6, K1, rep from * to last 3 [5: 6: 6: 0] sts, P3 [5: 6: 6: 0].
Row 13: (Inc in first st) 1 [0: 0: 0: 0] times, K2 [2: 1: 1: 0], (yfwd, sl 1, K1, psso, K1) 0 [1: 0: 0: 0] times, (K2tog, yfwd, yfwd, sl 1, K1, psso, K1) 0 [0: 1: 1: 0] times, *P1, K1, K2tog, (yfwd) twice, sl 1, K1, psso, K1, rep from * to last 4 [6: 0: 0: 1] sts, P1 [1: 0: 0: 1], (K1, K2tog, yfwd) 0 [1: 0: 0: 0] times, K2 [2: 0: 0: 0], (inc in last st) 1 [0: 0: 0: 0] times. 44 [46: 48: 48: 50] sts.
Row 14: P4 [5: 0: 0: 0], K1 [1: 0: 0: 1], *P2, (P1, P1 tbl) into double yfwd of previous row, P2, K1, rep from * to last 4 [5: 6: 6: 0] sts, P4 [5: 2: 2: 0], (P1 and P1 tbl into double yfwd of previous row, P2) 0 [0: 1: 1: 0] times.
Row 15: K4 [5: 6: 6: 0], (P1, C6F) 0 [0: 0: 0: 1] times, *P1, K1, yfwd, K2tog, sl 1, K1, psso, yfwd, K1, P1, C6F, rep from * to last 12 [13: 14: 14: 1] sts, P1, (K1, K2tog, yfwd, sl 1, K1, psso, yfwd, K1, P1) 1 [1: 1: 1: 0] times, K4 [5: 6: 6: 0].
Row 16: P4 [5: 6: 6: 0], K1, *P6, K1, rep from * to last 4 [5: 6: 6: 0] sts, P4 [5: 6: 6: 0].
These 16 rows form patt and beg sleeve shaping.
Cont in patt, shaping sides by inc 1 st at each end of 5th [next: next: next: next] and every foll 8th [8th: 6th: 6th: 6th] row to 68 [72: 56: 72: 82] sts, then on every foll - [-: 8th: 8th: 8th] row until there are - [-: 76: 80: 84] sts, taking inc sts into patt.
Cont straight until sleeve meas 44 [45: 46: 46: 46] cm, ending with RS facing for next row.
Shape top
Keeping patt correct, cast off 4 [5: 6: 7: 8] sts at beg of next 2 rows. 60 [62: 64: 66: 68] sts.
Dec 1 st at each end of next 5 rows, then on foll 3 alt rows, then on 3 foll 4th rows. 38 [40: 42: 44: 46] sts.
Work 1 row.
Dec 1 st at each end of next and every foll alt row until 32 sts rem, then on foll 5 rows, ending with RS facing for next row. 22 sts.
Cast off 4 sts at beg of next 2 rows.
Cast off rem 14 sts.

MAKING UP
Press as described on the information page.
Join both shoulder seams using back stitch, or mattress stitch if preferred.
Back opening borders (both alike)
With RS facing and using 3¼mm (US 3) needles, pick up and knit 120 [125: 130: 135: 139] sts evenly along entire back opening edge, between cast-on edge and neck shaping.
Work in g st for 2 rows, ending with **WS** facing for next row.
Cast off knitwise (on **WS**).
Neckband
With RS facing and using 3¼mm (US 3) needles, beg and ending at cast-off edges of back opening borders, pick up and knit 45 [45: 46:

46: 48] sts up left side of back neck, 14 [14: 16: 16: 18] sts down left side of front neck, 34 sts from front, 14 [14: 16: 16: 18] sts up right side of front neck, then 45 [45: 46: 46: 48] sts down right side of back neck. 152 [152: 158: 158: 166] sts.
Work in g st for 2 rows, ending with **WS** facing for next row.
Cast off knitwise (on **WS**).
See information page for finishing instructions, setting in sleeves using the set-in method. Overlap back opening edges so that markers on back neck cast-off edges match. Attach buttons to RS of left back approx 6.5 cm either side of marker and 2 cm below upper edge. Fasten right back over these buttons, using "holes" of patt as buttonholes.

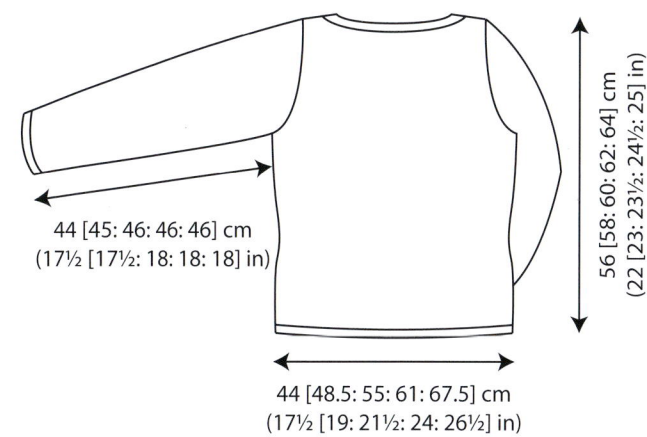

Cabernet *
By Lisa Richardson

Main Image Page 19

SIZES

S	M	L	XL	XXL	
To fit bust					
81-86	91-97	102-107	112-117	122-127	cm
32-34	36-38	40-42	44-46	48-50	in

YARN
Kidsilk Haze and Anchor Artiste Metallic

A Kidsilk Haze Brick 649
  7   7   8   9   10   x 25gm
B Kidsilk Haze Fudge 658
  7   8   9   9   10   x 25gm
C Metallic Bronze 314
  11   12   13   14   16   x 25gm

NEEDLES
1 pair 5mm (no 6) (US 8) needles
1 pair 6mm (no 4) (US 10) needles

TENSION
16 sts and 23 rows to 10 cm measured over patt using 6mm (US 10) needles and one strand each of yarns A, B and C held together.

BACK
Using 5mm (US 8) needles and one strand each of yarns A, B and C held together cast on 83 [91: 103: 111: 123] sts.
Row 1 (RS): K3 [3: 1: 1: 3], *P1, K3, rep from * to last 0 [0: 2: 2: 0] sts, (P1, K1) 0 [0: 1: 1: 0] times.
Row 2: P1 [1: 3: 3: 1], *K1, P3, rep from * to last 2 [2: 0: 0: 2] sts, (K1, P1) 1 [1: 0: 0: 1] times.
These 2 rows form patt.
Work in patt for a further 6 rows, ending with RS facing for next row.
Change to 6mm (US 10) needles.
Cont in patt until back meas 54 [55: 56: 57: 58] cm, ending with RS facing for next row.
Shape armholes
Keeping patt correct, cast off 4 [5: 6: 7: 8] sts at beg of next 2 rows.

75 [81: 91: 97: 107] sts.
Dec 1 st at each end of next 3 [5: 5: 5: 7] rows, then on foll 4 [3: 6: 7: 7] alt rows. 61 [65: 69: 73: 79] sts.
Cont straight until armhole meas 22 [23: 24: 25: 26] cm, ending with RS facing for next row.

Shape shoulders and back neck
Next row (RS): Cast off 5 [6: 6: 7: 8] sts, patt until there are 14 [15: 16: 17: 18] sts on right needle and turn, leaving rem sts on a holder.
Work each side of neck separately.
Dec 1 st at neck edge of next 3 rows, ending with RS facing for next row, **and at same time** cast off 5 [6: 6: 7: 8] sts at beg of 2nd row.
Cast off rem 6 [6: 7: 7: 7] sts.
With RS facing, rejoin yarns to rem sts, cast off centre 23 [23: 25: 25: 27] sts, patt to end.
Complete to match first side, reversing shapings.

LEFT FRONT
Using 5mm (US 8) needles and one strand each of yarns A, B and C held together cast on 50 [54: 60: 64: 70] sts.
Row 1 (RS): K3 [3: 1: 1: 3], *P1, K3, rep from * to last 3 sts, P1, K2.
Row 2: *K1, P3, rep from * to last 2 [2: 0: 0: 2] sts, (K1, P1) 1 [1: 0: 0: 1] times.
These 2 rows form patt.
Work in patt for a further 6 rows, ending with RS facing for next row.
Change to 6mm (US 10) needles.
Cont in patt until 42 rows less have been worked than on back to beg of armhole shaping, ending with RS facing for next row.

Shape for collar
Row 1 (RS): Patt to last 2 sts, inc once in each of last 2 sts. 52 [56: 62: 66: 72] sts.
Row 2: K2, place marker on needle, patt to end.
From this point onwards, sts one side of marker form left front, and sts other side of marker form collar.
Move marker one st closer to side seam edge. (3 sts in collar section.)
Row 3: Patt to marker, slip marker onto right needle, P2, K1.
Row 4: K2, P1, slip marker onto right needle, patt to end.
Move marker one st closer to side seam edge.
Row 5: Patt to marker, slip marker onto right needle, P3, K1.
Row 6: K2, P1, K1, slip marker onto right needle, patt to end.
Move marker one st closer to side seam edge.
Row 7: Patt to marker, slip marker onto right needle, M1 (for collar inc), K1, P3, K1. 53 [57: 63: 67: 73] sts.
Row 8: K2, P1, K3, slip marker onto right needle, patt to end.
Move marker one st closer to side seam edge.
Row 9: Patt to marker, slip marker onto right needle, P2, K1, P3, K1.
Row 10: K2, P1, K3, P1, slip marker onto right needle, patt to end.
Keeping sts correct as now set (with collar sts in same patt as left front sts **BUT** with RS of this section being WS of other section), cont as folls:
Move marker one st closer to side seam edge.
Work 4 rows.
Move marker one st closer to side seam edge.
Row 15: Patt to marker, slip marker onto right needle, M1 (for collar inc), patt to end. 54 [58: 64: 68: 74] sts.
Work 3 rows.
Moving marker one st closer to side seam edge before next and every foll 4th row, inc 1 st for collar on 5th and 2 foll 8th rows, taking inc sts into patt. 57 [61: 67: 71: 77] sts.
Work 3 rows, ending with RS facing for next row.

Shape armhole
Keeping both sections of patt correct and still moving marker one st closer to side seam/armhole edge before next and every foll 4th row, cont as folls:
Cast off 4 [5: 6: 7: 8] sts at beg of next row. 53 [56: 61: 64: 69] sts.
Work 1 row.
Dec 1 st at armhole edge of next 3 [5: 5: 5: 7] rows, then on foll 4 [3: 6: 7: 7] alt rows **and at same time** inc 1 st for collar on 3rd and 1 [1: 1: 2: 2] foll 8th rows. 48 [50: 52: 55: 58] sts.
Still moving marker 1 st closer to armhole edge before every 4th row as set, inc 1 st for collar on 8th [8th: 2nd: 8th: 6th] and 2 [2: 2: 1: 1] foll 8th rows. 51 [53: 55: 57: 60] sts.
Cont to move marker one st closer to armhole edge before every foll 4th row as set until there are 16 [18: 19: 21: 23] sts in patt on armhole edge side of marker and 35 [35: 36: 36: 37] sts in patt for collar on other side of marker.
Cont straight until left front matches back to beg of shoulder shaping, ending with RS facing for next row.

Shape shoulder
Keeping patt correct, cast off 5 [6: 6: 7: 8] sts at beg of next and foll alt row, then 6 [6: 7: 7: 7] sts at beg of foll alt row. 35 [35: 36: 36: 37] sts.
Remove marker and cont on these collar sts only for back neck collar extension as folls:
Work 2 rows.
Next row (RS of collar, WS of front): Patt to last 4 sts, wrap next st (by slipping next st from left needle onto right needle, taking yarn to opposite side of work between needles and then slipping same st back onto left needle - when working back across wrapped sts work the wrapped st and the wrapping loop tog as one st) and turn.
Next row: Patt to end.
Rep last 4 rows 4 [4: 5: 5: 6] times more.
Work 2 rows, ending with RS of collar facing for next row.
Cast off.

RIGHT FRONT
Using 5mm (US 8) needles and one strand each of yarns A, B and C held together cast on 50 [54: 60: 64: 70] sts.
Row 1 (RS): K2, P1, *K3, P1, rep from * to last 3 [3: 1: 1: 3] sts, K3 [3: 1: 1: 3].
Row 2: (P1, K1) 1 [1: 0: 0: 1] times, *P3, K1, rep from * to end.
These 2 rows form patt.
Work in patt for a further 6 rows, ending with RS facing for next row.
Change to 6mm (US 10) needles.
Cont in patt until 42 rows less have been worked than on back to beg of armhole shaping, ending with RS facing for next row.

Shape for collar
Row 1 (RS): Inc once in each of first 2 sts, patt to end.

52 [56: 62: 66: 72] sts.

Row 2: Patt to last 2 sts, place marker on needle, K2.

From this point onwards, sts one side of marker form right front, and sts other side of marker form collar.

Move marker one st closer to side seam edge. (3 sts in collar section.)

Row 3: K1, P2, slip marker onto right needle, patt to end.

Row 4: Patt to marker, slip marker onto right needle, P1, K2.

Move marker one st closer to side seam edge.

Row 5: K1, P3, slip marker onto right needle, patt to end.

Row 6: Patt to marker, slip marker onto right needle, K1, P1, K2.

Move marker one st closer to side seam edge.

Row 7: K1, P3, K1, M1 (for collar inc), slip marker onto right needle, patt to end. 53 [57: 63: 67: 73] sts.

Row 8: Patt to marker, slip marker onto right needle, K3, P1, K2.

Move marker one st closer to side seam edge.

Row 9: K1, P3, K1, P2, slip marker onto right needle, patt to end.

Row 10: Patt to marker, slip marker onto right needle, P1, K3, P1, K2.

Keeping sts correct as now set (with collar sts in same patt as right front sts **BUT** with RS of this section being WS of other section), complete to match left front, reversing shapings.

SLEEVES

Using 5mm (US 8) needles and one strand each of yarns A, B and C held together cast on 39 [41: 43: 43: 45] sts.

Row 1 (RS): K3 [0: 1: 1: 2], *P1, K3, rep from * to last 0 [1: 2: 2: 3] sts, P0 [1: 1: 1: 1], K0 [0: 1: 1: 2].

Row 2: P1 [2: 3: 3: 0], *K1, P3, rep from * to last 2 [3: 0: 0: 1] sts, K1 [1: 0: 0: 1], P1 [2: 0: 0: 0].

These 2 rows form patt.

Work in patt for a further 6 rows, ending with RS facing for next row.

Change to 6mm (US 10) needles.

Cont in patt, shaping sides by inc 1 st at each end of 7th [7th: 7th: 5th: 5th] and every foll 8th [8th: 8th: 6th: 6th] row to 43 [53: 63: 57: 67] sts, then on every foll 10th [10th: 10th: 8th: 8th] row until there are 57 [61: 65: 69: 73] sts, taking inc sts into patt.

Cont straight until sleeve meas 45 [46: 47: 47: 47] cm, ending with RS facing for next row.

Shape top

Keeping patt correct, cast off 4 [5: 6: 7: 8] sts at beg of next 2 rows.

49 [51: 53: 55: 57] sts.

Dec 1 st at each end of next 3 rows, then on every foll alt row until 27 sts rem, then on foll 7 rows, ending with RS facing for next row.

Cast off rem 13 sts.

MAKING UP

Press as described on the information page.

Join both shoulder seams using back stitch, or mattress stitch if preferred.

Join cast-off ends of back neck collar extensions, then sew row-end edge in place to back neck edge, easing in slight fullness.

See information page for finishing instructions, setting in sleeves using the set-in method.

Belt

Using 5mm (US 8) needles and one strand each of yarns A, B and C held together cast on 11 sts.

Row 1 (RS): K2, (P1, K1) 4 times, K1.

Row 2: K1, (P1, K1) 5 times.

These 2 rows form rib.

Cont in rib until belt meas 150 [160: 170: 180: 190] cm, ending with RS facing for next row.

Cast off in rib.

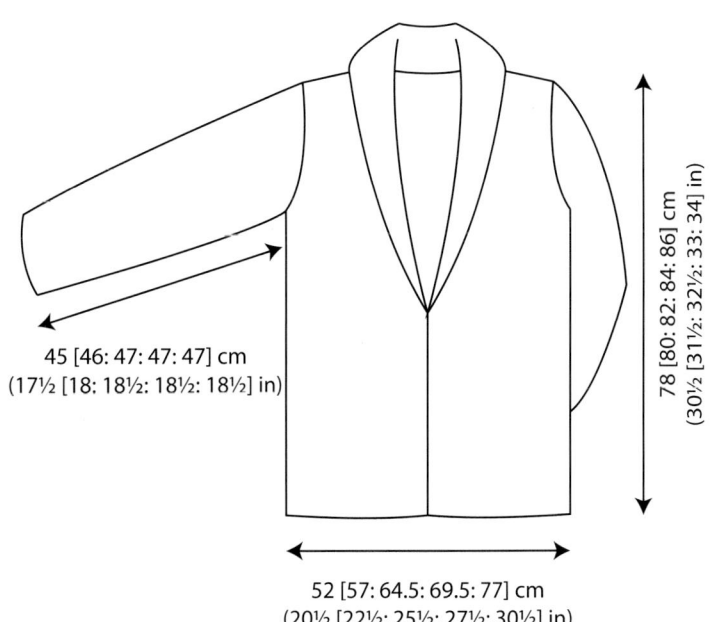

45 [46: 47: 47: 47] cm
(17½ [18: 18½: 18½: 18½] in)

78 [80: 82: 84: 86] cm
(30½ [31½: 32½: 33: 34] in)

52 [57: 64.5: 69.5: 77] cm
(20½ [22½: 25½: 27½: 30½] in)

Chablis ★★

By Marie Wallin

Main Image Page 28

SIZES

S	M	L	XL	XXL	
To fit bust					
81-86	91-97	102-107	112-117	122-127	cm
32-34	36-38	40-42	44-46	48-50	in

YARN

Kidsilk Haze and Fine Lace

A Kidsilk Haze Majestic 589

5	5	6	7	7	x 25gm

B Fine Lace Cobweb 922

1	1	1	1	1	x 50gm

NEEDLES

1 pair 2¼mm (no 13) (US 1) needles
1 pair 2¾mm (no 12) (US 2) needles

BUTTONS – 1 x BN1365 from Bedecked. Please see information page for contact details.

BEADS – approx 500 [530: 570: 620: 660] small glass beads.

TENSION

36 sts and 40 rows to 10 cm measured over st st using 2¾mm (US 2) needles and yarn A.

SPECIAL ABBREVIATION

bead 1 = place a bead by taking yarn to RS of work and slipping bead up next to st just worked, slip next st purlwise from left needle to right needle and take yarn back to WS of work, leaving bead sitting in front of slipped st on RS.

Beading note: Before starting to knit, thread beads onto yarn B. To do this, thread a fine sewing needle (one that will easily pass through the beads) with sewing thread. Knot ends of thread and then pass end of yarn through this loop. Thread a bead onto sewing thread and then gently slide it along and onto knitting yarn. Continue in this way until required number of beads are on yarn. Do not place beads on edge sts of rows as this will interfere with seaming.

BACK

Using 2¼mm (US 1) needles and yarn A cast on 151 [169: 191: 213: 237] sts.
Row 1 (RS): K1, *P1, K1, rep from * to end.
Row 2: As row 1.
These 2 rows form moss st.
Work in moss st for a further 2 rows, ending with RS facing for next row.
Change to 2¾mm (US 2) needles.
Beg with a K row, now work in st st as folls:
Dec 1 st at each end of 5th and 6 foll 6th rows. 137 [155: 177: 199: 223] sts.
Work 19 rows, ending with RS facing for next row.
Inc 1 st at each end of next and 6 foll 6th rows. 151 [169: 191: 213: 237] sts.
Cont straight until back meas 29 [30: 31: 32: 33] cm, ending with RS facing for next row.
Now work in yoke patt as folls:
Break off yarn A and join in yarn B.
Row 1 (RS): K1 [2: 1: 0: 0], K2tog, yfwd, *K1, yfwd, sl 1, K1, psso, K1, bead 1, K1, K2tog, yfwd, rep from * to last 4 [5: 4: 3: 3] sts, K1, yfwd, sl 1, K1, psso, K1 [2: 1: 0: 0].
Row 2: Purl.
Row 3: K0 [1: 0: 2: 2], (K2tog, yfwd, K1) 1 [1: 1: 0: 0] times, *K2, yfwd, sl 1, K1, psso, K1, K2tog, yfwd, K1, rep from * to last 4 [5: 4: 3: 3] sts, (K2, yfwd, sl 1, K1, psso) 1 [1: 1: 0: 0] times, K0 [1: 0: 3: 3].
Row 4: Purl.
Row 5: (K2tog, yfwd) 0 [1: 0: 0: 0] times, K3 [2: 3: 2: 2], *bead 1, K2, yfwd, sl 1, K2tog, psso, yfwd, K2, rep from * to last 4 [5: 4: 3: 3] sts, bead 1, K3 [2: 3: 2: 2], (yfwd, sl 1, K1, psso) 0 [1: 0: 0: 0] times.
Row 6: Purl.
Row 7: K1 [2: 1: 2: 2], (yfwd, sl 1, K1, psso) 1 [1: 1: 0: 0] times, *K1, K2tog, yfwd, K3, yfwd, sl 1, K1, psso, rep from * to last 4 [5: 4: 3: 3] sts, (K1, K2tog, yfwd) 1 [1: 1: 0: 0] times, K1 [2: 1: 3: 3].
Row 8: Purl.
Row 9: K2 [3: 2: 1: 1], *yfwd, sl 1, K2tog, psso, yfwd, K2, bead 1, K2, rep from * to last 5 [6: 5: 4: 4] sts, yfwd, sl 1, K2tog, psso, yfwd, K2 [3: 2: 1: 1].
Row 10: Purl.
Break off yarn B and join in yarn A.

Beg with a K row, work in st st for 16 rows, ending with RS facing for next row. (Back should meas approx 35 [36: 37: 38: 39] cm.)

Shape armholes

Cast off 6 [8: 10: 12: 14] sts at beg of next 2 rows. 139 [153: 171: 189: 209] sts.
Dec 1 st at each end of next 6 rows, ending with RS facing for next row. 127 [141: 159: 177: 197] sts.
Last 34 rows form yoke patt – 10 rows in beaded lace patt using yarn B followed by 24 rows in st st using yarn A.
Keeping yoke patt correct throughout, cont as folls:
Dec 1 st at each end of next 1 [1: 3: 5: 9] rows, then on foll 5 [8: 10: 11: 11] alt rows. 115 [123: 133: 145: 157] sts.★★
Cont straight until armhole meas 9 [10: 11: 12: 13] cm, ending with RS facing for next row.

Divide for back opening

Next row (RS): Patt 57 [61: 66: 72: 78] sts and turn, leaving rem sts on a holder.
Work each side of neck separately.
Cont straight until armhole meas 17 [18: 19: 20: 21] cm, ending with **WS** facing for next row.

Shape back neck

Keeping patt correct, cast off 23 [23: 25: 25: 27] sts at beg of next row. 34 [38: 41: 47: 51] sts.
Dec 1 st at neck edge of next 2 rows, ending with RS facing for next row. 32 [36: 39: 45: 49] sts.

Shape shoulder

Cast off 10 [11: 12: 14: 15] sts at beg of next and foll alt row **and at same time** dec 1 st at neck edge of next 3 rows.
Work 1 row.
Cast off rem 9 [11: 12: 14: 16] sts.
With RS facing, rejoin appropriate yarn to rem sts, cast off centre st, patt to end.
Complete to match first side, reversing shapings.

FRONT

Work as given for back to ★★.
Cont straight until 36 [36: 40: 40: 42] rows less have been worked than on back to beg of shoulder shaping, ending with RS facing for next row.

Shape front neck

Next row (RS): Patt 44 [48: 53: 59: 65] sts and turn, leaving rem sts on a holder.
Work each side of neck separately.
Keeping patt correct, dec 1 st at neck edge of next 8 [8: 8: 8: 10] rows, then on foll 4 [4: 6: 6: 6] alt rows, then on 2 foll 4th rows, then on foll 6th row. 29 [33: 36: 42: 46] sts.
Work 5 rows, ending with RS facing for next row.

Shape shoulder

Cast off 10 [11: 12: 14: 15] sts at beg of next and foll alt row.
Work 1 row.
Cast off rem 9 [11: 12: 14: 16] sts.
With RS facing, rejoin appropriate yarn to rem sts, cast off centre 27 sts, patt to end.
Complete to match first side, reversing shapings.

SLEEVES

Using 2¼mm (US 1) needles and yarn A cast on 115 [121: 125: 125: 131] sts.
Work in moss st as given for back for 4 rows, ending with RS facing for next row.
Change to 2¾mm (US 2) needles.
Beg with a K row, work in st st until sleeve meas 7.5 cm, ending with RS facing for next row.
Next row (RS): K1 [0: 2: 2: 1], (K1, K2tog, K1) 28 [30: 30: 30: 32] times, K2 [1: 3: 3: 2]. 87 [91: 95: 95: 99] sts.
Next row: Purl.
Break off yarn A and join in yarn B.
Row 1 (RS): K1, (K2tog, yfwd) 1 [0: 1: 1: 0] times, *K1, yfwd, sl 1, K1, psso, K1, bead 1, K1, K2tog, yfwd, rep from * to last 4 [2: 4: 4: 2] sts, (K1, yfwd, sl 1, K1, psso) 1 [0: 1: 1: 0] times, K1 [2: 1: 1: 2].
Row 2: Purl.
Row 3: (K2tog, yfwd) 1 [0: 1: 1: 0] times, K1, *K2, yfwd, sl 1, K1, psso, K1, K2tog, yfwd, K1, rep from * to last 4 [2: 4: 4: 2] sts, K2, (yfwd, sl 1, K1, psso) 1 [0: 1: 1: 0] times.
Row 4: Purl.
Row 5: K3 [1: 3: 3: 1], *bead 1, K2, yfwd, sl 1, K2tog, psso, yfwd, K2, rep from * to last 4 [2: 4: 4: 2] sts, bead 1, K3 [1: 3: 3: 1].
Row 6: Purl.
Row 7: K1, (yfwd, sl 1, K1, psso) 1 [0: 1: 1: 0] times, *K1, K2tog, yfwd, K3, yfwd, sl 1, K1, psso, rep from * to last 4 [2: 4: 4: 2] sts, (K1, K2tog, yfwd) 1 [0: 1: 1: 0] times, K1 [2: 1: 1: 2].
Row 8: Purl.
Row 9: (K1, K2tog, yfwd, K2, bead 1) 0 [1: 0: 0: 1] times, K2, *yfwd, sl 1, K2tog, psso, yfwd, K2, bead 1, K2, rep from * to last 5 [3: 5: 5: 3] sts, yfwd, (sl 1, K2tog, psso, yfwd, K2) 1 [0: 1: 1: 0] times, (sl 1, K1, psso, K1) 0 [1: 0: 0: 1] times.
Row 10: Purl.
Break off yarn B and join in yarn A.
Beg with a K row, work in st st, shaping sides by inc 1 st at each end of next and foll 0 [0: 0: 6: 8] alt rows, then on every foll 4th row until there are 123 [129: 135: 141: 147] sts.
Work 3 rows, ending with RS facing for next row.
Now work in yoke patt as folls:
Break off yarn A and join in yarn B.
Row 1 (RS): K1 [2: 1: 0: 1], (K2tog, yfwd) 0 [1: 1: 1: 0] times, *K1, yfwd, sl 1, K1, psso, K1, bead 1, K1, K2tog, yfwd, rep from * to last 2 [5: 4: 3: 2] sts, (K1, yfwd, sl 1, K1, psso) 0 [1: 1: 1: 0] times, K2 [2: 1: 0: 2].
Row 2: Purl.
Row 3: K1 [1: 0: 2: 1], (K2tog, yfwd, K1) 0 [1: 1: 0: 0] times, *K2, yfwd, sl 1, K1, psso, K1, K2tog, yfwd, K1, rep from * to last 2 [5: 4: 3: 2] sts, (K2, yfwd, sl 1, K1, psso) 0 [1: 1: 0: 0] times, K2 [1: 0: 3: 2].
Row 4: Purl.
Row 5: K1 [0: 3: 2: 1], (K2tog, yfwd, K2) 0 [1: 0: 0: 0] times, *bead 1, K2, yfwd, sl 1, K2tog, psso, yfwd, K2, rep from * to last 2 [5: 4: 3: 2] sts, bead 1, (K2, yfwd, sl 1, K1, psso) 0 [1: 0: 0: 0] times, K1 [0: 3: 2: 1].
Row 6: Purl.
Row 7: K1 [2: 1: 2: 1], (yfwd, sl 1, K1, psso) 0 [1: 1: 0: 0] times, *K1,

K2tog, yfwd, K3, yfwd, sl 1, K1, psso, rep from * to last 2 [5: 4: 3: 2] sts, (K1, K2tog, yfwd) 0 [1: 1: 0: 0] times, K2 [2: 1: 3: 2].
Row 8: Purl.
Row 9: K1 [3: 2: 1: 1], (K2tog, yfwd, K2, bead 1, K2) 1 [0: 0: 0: 1] times, *yfwd, sl 1, K2tog, psso, yfwd, K2, bead 1, K2, rep from * to last 3 [6: 5: 4: 3] sts, (yfwd, sl 1, K1, psso) 1 [0: 0: 0: 1] times, (yfwd, sl 1, K2tog, psso, yfwd) 0 [1: 1: 1: 0] times, K1 [3: 2: 1: 1].
Row 10: Purl.
Break off yarn B and join in yarn A.
Beg with a K row, work in st st for 16 rows, ending with RS facing for next row. (Sleeve should meas approx 34 [35: 36: 36: 36] cm.)
Last 26 rows **set position** of yoke patt as given for back - 10 rows in beaded lace patt using yarn B followed by 24 rows in st st using yarn A.
Shape top
Keeping yoke patt correct as now set (by working rem 8 rows in st st and then starting rep again with beaded lace patt), cast off 6 [8: 10: 12: 14] sts at beg of next 2 rows. 111 [113: 115: 117: 119] sts.
Dec 1 st at each end of next 9 rows, then on every foll alt row until 81 sts rem, then on foll 19 rows, ending with RS facing for next row. 43 sts. (**Note**: After 2nd band of beaded lace patt, complete sleeve top in st st using yarn A only.)
Cast off 5 sts at beg of next 4 rows.
Cast off rem 23 sts.

MAKING UP
Press as described on the information page.
Join both shoulder seams using back stitch, or mattress stitch if preferred.
Back opening edging
With RS facing, using 2¼mm (US 1) needles and yarn A, beg and ending at neck edge, pick up and knit 29 sts down right side of back opening, then 29 sts up left side of back opening. 58 sts.
Cast off knitwise (on **WS**).
Neckband
With RS facing, using 2¼mm (US 1) needles and yarn A, beg and ending at back opening edges, pick up and knit 29 [29: 31: 31: 33] sts from left side of back neck, 36 [36: 40: 40: 44] sts down left side of front neck, 27 sts from front, 36 [36: 40: 40: 44] sts up right side of front neck, then 29 [29: 31: 31: 33] sts from right side of back neck.
157 [157: 169: 169: 181] sts.
Work in moss st as given for back for 3 rows, ending with RS facing for next row.
Cast off in moss st.
See information page for finishing instructions, setting in sleeves using the set-in method. Make buttonloop at one end of neckband and attach button to other end to fasten back neck opening.

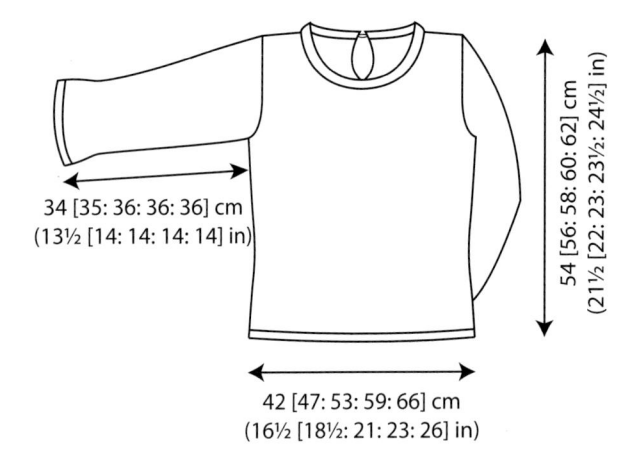

34 [35: 36: 36: 36] cm
(13½ [14: 14: 14: 14] in)

54 [56: 58: 60: 62] cm
(21½ [22: 23: 23½: 24½] in)

42 [47: 53: 59: 66] cm
(16½ [18½: 21: 23: 26] in)

Champagne ★★
By Marie Wallin

Main Image Page 14

SIZES

S	M	L	XL	XXL	
To fit bust					
81-86	91-97	102-107	112-117	122-127	cm
32-34	36-38	40-42	44-46	48-50	in

YARN

Kidsilk Haze and Fine Lace

A Kidsilk Haze Majestic 589

4	4	5	5	6	x 25gm

B Fine Lace Gunmetal 929

2	2	2	2	2	x 50gm

NEEDLES
1 pair 2¾mm (no 12) (US 2) needles
1 pair 3¼mm (no 10) (US 3) needles
2¾mm (no 12) (US 2) circular needle 80 cm long
1.75mm (no 15) (US 5 steel) crochet hook

BUTTONS - 1 x BN1365 from Bedecked. Please see information page for contact details.

TENSION
25 sts and 34 rows to 10 cm measured over st st using 3¼mm (US 3) needles and yarn A.

CROCHET ABBREVIATIONS
picot cluster = 4 ch, ss to 4th ch from hook, (3 ch, 1 ss into same place as last ss) twice; **ch** = chain; **dc** = double crochet; **htr** = half treble; **sp(s)** = space(s); **ss** = slip stitch; **tr** = treble.

BACK
Using 2¾mm (US 2) needles and yarn A cast on 105 [117: 133: 147: 165] sts.
Work in g st for 4 rows, ending with RS facing for next row.
Change to 3¼mm (US 3) needles.
Beg with a K row, work in st st, shaping side seams by dec 1 st at each end of 7th and 4 foll 6th rows. 95 [107: 123: 137: 155] sts.
Cont straight until back meas 17 [18: 19: 20: 21] cm, ending with RS facing for next row.
Inc 1 st at each end of next and 4 foll 10th rows. 105 [117: 133: 147: 165] sts.
Work 17 rows, ending with RS facing for next row. (Back should meas 34 [35: 36: 37: 38] cm.)
Shape armholes
Cast off 4 [5: 6: 7: 8] sts at beg of next 2 rows. 97 [107: 121: 133: 149] sts.
Dec 1 st at each end of next 5 [7: 7: 9: 11] rows, then on foll 3 [4: 7: 7: 9] alt rows. 81 [85: 93: 101: 109] sts.
Cont straight until armhole meas 18 [19: 20: 21: 22] cm, ending with RS facing for next row.
Shape shoulders and back neck
Next row (RS): Cast off 5 [6: 7: 8: 9] sts, K until there are 13 [14: 16: 19: 21] sts on right needle and turn, leaving rem sts on a holder.
Work each side of neck separately.
Dec 1 st at neck edge of next 3 rows, ending with RS facing for next row, **and at same time** cast off 5 [6: 7: 8: 9] sts at beg of 2nd row.
Cast off rem 5 [5: 6: 8: 9] sts.
With RS facing, rejoin yarn to rem sts, cast off centre 45 [45: 47: 47: 49] sts, K to end.
Complete to match first side, reversing shapings.

LEFT FRONT
Using 2¾mm (US 2) needles and yarn A cast on 100 [112: 128: 142: 160] sts.
Work in g st for 4 rows, ending with RS facing for next row.
Change to 3¼mm (US 3) needles.
Next row (RS): Knit.
Next row: K2, P to end.
These 2 rows set the sts.
Keeping sts correct as now set, dec 1 st at beg of 5th and 4 foll 6th rows. 95 [107: 123: 137: 155] sts.
Cont straight until 17 rows less have been worked than on back to first side seam increase, ending with **WS** facing for next row.
Shape front slope
Cast off 15 sts at beg of next row. 80 [92: 108: 122: 140] sts.
Dec 1 st at front slope edge of next 11 [21: 35: 45: 63] rows, then on foll 31 [26: 19: 14: 5] alt rows **and at same time** inc 1 st at side seam edge of 17th and 4 foll 10th rows. 43 [50: 59: 68: 77] sts.
Work 1 row, ending with RS facing for next row.
Shape armhole
Cast off 4 [5: 6: 7: 8] sts at beg and dec 1 st at end of next row. 38 [44: 52: 60: 68] sts.
Work 1 row.

Dec 1 st at armhole edge of next 5 [7: 7: 9: 11] rows, then on foll 3 [4: 7: 7: 9] alt rows **and at same time** dec 1 st at front slope edge of next and foll 5 [7: 10: 11: 14] alt rows. 24 [25: 27: 32: 33] sts.
Dec 1 st at front slope edge **only** on 2nd [2nd: 2nd: 2nd: 4th] and foll 2 [1: 0: 1: 0] alt rows, then on 3 [3: 3: 3: 2] foll 4th rows, then on 2 foll 6th rows, then on foll 8th row. 15 [17: 20: 24: 27] sts.
Cont straight until left front matches back to beg of shoulder shaping, ending with RS facing for next row.

Shape shoulder
Cast off 5 [6: 7: 8: 9] sts at beg of next and foll alt row.
Work 1 row.
Cast off rem 5 [5: 6: 8: 9] sts.

RIGHT FRONT
Using 2¾mm (US 2) needles and yarn A cast on 85 [97: 113: 127: 145] sts.
Work in g st for 4 rows, ending with RS facing for next row.
Change to 3¼mm (US 3) needles.
Beg with a K row, work in st st as folls:
Work 2 rows, ending with RS facing for next row.
**Next row (RS): K to last 3 sts, wrap next st (by slipping next st from left needle onto right needle, taking yarn to opposite side of work between needles and then slipping same st back onto left needle - when working back across wrapped sts work the wrapped st and the wrapping loop tog as one st) and turn.
Next row: P to end.
Next row (RS): K to last 8 sts, wrap next st and turn.
Next row: P to end.**
Work 4 rows.
Rep from ** to ** once more.
Work 4 rows, dec 1 st at end of first of these rows.
84 [96: 112: 126: 144] sts.
Rep from ** to ** once more.
Work 4 rows, dec 1 st at end of 3rd of these rows.
83 [95: 111: 125: 143] sts.
Rep from ** to ** once more.
Work 4 rows.
***Next row (RS): K to last 3 sts, wrap next st and turn.
Next row: P to end.***
Work 4 rows, dec 1 st at end of first of these rows.
82 [94: 110: 124: 142] sts.
Rep from *** to *** once more.
Work 4 rows, dec 1 st at end of 3rd of these rows.
81 [93: 109: 123: 141] sts.
Rep from *** to *** once more.
Work 4 rows.
Rep from *** to *** once more.
Work 4 rows, dec 1 st at end of first of these rows.
80 [92: 108: 122: 140] sts.
Rep from *** to *** once more.
Measuring at side seam edge (as front opening edge is 26 rows longer), cont straight until 16 rows less have been worked than on back to first side seam increase, ending with RS facing for next row.

Shape front slope
Place marker at end of last row - this denotes beg of front slope.
Dec 1 st at front slope edge of next 11 [21: 35: 45: 63] rows, then on foll 31 [26: 19: 14: 5] alt rows **and at same time** inc 1 st at side seam edge of 17th and 4 foll 10th rows. 43 [50: 59: 68: 77] sts.
Complete to match left front, reversing shapings.

SLEEVES
Using 2¾mm (US 2) needles and yarn A cast on 65 [69: 73: 77: 81] sts.
Work in g st for 4 rows, ending with RS facing for next row.
Change to 3¼mm (US 3) needles.
Beg with a K row, work in st st, shaping sides by inc 1 st at each end of 3rd and 5 foll 4th rows, then on 4 foll 6th rows. 85 [89: 93: 97: 101] sts.
Cont straight until sleeve meas 18 cm, ending with RS facing for next row.

Shape top
Cast off 4 [5: 6: 7: 8] sts at beg of next 2 rows. 77 [79: 81: 83: 85] sts.
Dec 1 st at each end of next 5 rows, then on every foll alt row until 47 sts rem, then on foll 11 rows, ending with RS facing for next row. 25 sts.
Cast off 4 sts at beg of next 2 rows.
Cast off rem 17 sts.

MAKING UP
Press as described on the information page.
Join both shoulder seams using back stitch, or mattress stitch if preferred.

Front band
With RS facing, using 2¾mm (US 2) circular needle and yarn A, beg at cast-on edge, pick up and knit 50 [53: 55: 58: 60] sts up right front opening edge to marker, move marker onto right needle, pick up and knit 136 [138: 142: 146: 148] sts up right front slope, 51 [51: 53: 53: 55] from back, then 151 [153: 157: 161: 163] sts down left front slope to straight row-end edge. 388 [395: 407: 418: 426] sts.
Row 1 (WS): K to marker, M1, slip marker onto right needle, (K3tog) 0 [1: 0: 1: 0] times, (K2tog, K3tog) 10 [10: 11: 11: 12] times. 359 [364: 375: 384: 391] sts.
Row 2: K to marker, slip marker onto right needle, M1, K to end. 360 [365: 376: 385: 392] sts.
Cast off knitwise (on **WS**).
See information page for finishing instructions, setting in sleeves using the set-in method. Make button loop at left front end of front band and attach button to inside of right side seam to correspond.

Basic motif
Using 1.75mm (US 5 steel) crochet hook and yarn B make 6 ch and join with a ss to form a ring.
Round 1 (RS): 1 ch (does NOT count as st), 12 dc into ring, ss to first dc. 12 sts.
Round 2: 3 ch (counts as first tr), 1 tr into st at base of 3 ch, 2 tr into each of next 11 dc, ss to top of 3 ch at beg of round. 24 sts.
Round 3: 1 ch (does NOT count as st), 1 dc into each st to end, ss to first dc. 24 sts.
Round 4: 1 ch (does NOT count as st), 1 dc into first dc, ★5 ch, miss 2 dc, 1 dc into next dc, rep from ★ to end, replacing dc at end of last rep with ss to first dc. 8 ch sps.
Round 5: 1 ch (does NOT count as st), 1 dc into first dc, ★(1 htr, 3 tr, 1 picot cluster, 3 tr and 1 htr) into next ch sp, 1 dc into next dc, rep from ★ to end, replacing dc at end of last rep with ss to first dc.
Round 6: 1 ch (does NOT count as st), 1 dc into first dc, ★7 ch, 1 dc into centre loop of next picot cluster, 7 ch, 1 dc into next dc, rep from ★ to end, replacing dc at end of last rep with ss to first dc.
Round 7: 1 ch (does NOT count as st), ★8 dc into next ch sp, 1 picot

cluster, 8 dc into next ch sp, rep from * to end, ss to first dc.
Fasten off.
Motif is an 8-pointed star shape. At tip of each point there is a picot cluster. Join motifs whilst working round 7 by replacing the central (3 ch) of one picot cluster with (1 ch, 1 ss into corresponding ch loop of adjacent picot cluster, 1 ch). Join motifs at 2 adjacent points, leaving 2 points free along each side between joined points. (First motif will have 6 free points and 2 joined points. 2nd motif will be joined to first motif at 2 points, then 2 free points, next 2 points will be joined to 3rd motif, and rem 2 points will remain free.)

Body trim
Make 13 basic motifs and sew on fronts as in photograph.

Ties (make 2)
Make and join a strip of basic motifs to form a strip approx 40 cm long. Sew one end of first tie to marked point along right front opening edge. Sew one end of other tie to RS of left side seam level with beg of front slope shaping.

18 cm (7 in)

54 [56: 58: 60: 62] cm (21 [22: 23: 23½: 24½] in)

42 [47: 53: 59: 66] cm (16½ [18½: 21: 23: 26] in)

Chardonnay ***
By Marie Wallin

Main Image Page 27

SIZES
	S	M	L	XL	XXL	
To fit bust						
	81-86	91-97	102-107	112-117	122-127	cm
	32-34	36-38	40-42	44-46	48-50	in

YARN
Kidsilk Haze

5	6	7	7	9	x 25gm

(photographed in Anthracite 639)

NEEDLES
1 pair 4mm (no 8) (US 6) needles
3¼mm (no 10) (US 3) circular needle 100 cm long

TENSION
22 sts and 35 rows to 10 cm measured over patt using 4mm (US 6) needles.

BODY
Using 4mm (US 6) needles cast on 133 [141: 159: 169: 187] sts.
Place blue markers at both ends of cast-on edge.
Beg and ending rows as indicated and repeating the 18 st patt rep 7 [7: 8: 9: 10] times across each row, and repeating the 86 row patt rep throughout, now work in patt from appropriate chart for size being knitted as folls:
Cont straight until work meas 22 [24.5: 27.5: 30.5: 34] cm, ending with RS facing for next row.
Place red markers at both ends of last row.
Keeping patt correct, cast on 48 [54: 61: 67: 75] sts at beg of next 2 rows. 229 [249: 281: 303: 337] sts.
Place 2nd set of blue markers at both ends of last row.
Cont straight until work meas 21 cm from 2nd set of blue markers, ending with RS facing for next row.

Divide for armhole openings
Next row (RS): Patt 48 [54: 61: 67: 75] sts and turn, leaving rem sts on a holder.
Work on this set of sts only for right front.

Cont straight until work meas 17 [18: 19: 20: 21] cm from dividing row, ending with RS facing for next row.

Cast off, placing yellow marker on first cast-off st and green marker on last cast-off st.

Shape back

With RS facing, rejoin yarn to rem sts, patt 133 [141: 159: 169: 187] sts and turn, leaving rem sts on holder.

Work on this set of sts **only** for back.

Cont straight until work meas 17 [18: 19: 20: 21] cm from dividing row, ending with RS facing for next row.

Place green markers at both ends of last row.

Cont straight until work meas 22 [24.5: 27.5: 30.5: 34] cm from green markers, ending with RS facing for next row.

Cast off, placing yellow markers on first and last cast-off sts.

Shape left front

With RS facing, rejoin yarn to rem sts, patt to end.

48 [54: 61: 67: 75] sts.

Cont straight until work meas 17 [18: 19: 20: 21] cm from dividing row, ending with RS facing for next row.

Cast off, placing green marker on first cast-off st and yellow marker on last cast-off st.

SLEEVES

Using 4mm (US 6) needles cast on 61 [61: 69: 69: 69] sts.

Beg and ending rows as indicated and repeating the 18 st patt rep 3 times across each row, and repeating the 86 row patt rep throughout, now work in patt from appropriate chart for size being knitted as folls:

Noting that for sizes M, XL and XXL chart to be followed is **NOT** same chart as used for body, work 10 [12: 10: 8: 8] rows, ending with RS facing for next row.

Keeping patt correct, dec 1 st at each end of next and 5 [4: 4: 4: 4] foll 10th [12th: 8th: 8th: 8th] rows, then on 0 [0: 2: 2: 2] foll 10th rows.

49 [51: 55: 55: 55] sts. (**Note**: Sleeve shaping is **NOT** shown on charts.)

Work 19 rows, ending with RS facing for next row.

Inc 1 st at each end of next and every foll 4th row to 79 [83: 87: 85: 85] sts, then on foll 0 [0: 0: 3: 5] alt rows, taking inc sts into patt.

79 [83: 87: 91: 95] sts.

Work 3 rows, ending with RS facing for next row. (Sleeve should meas approx 40 [41: 42: 42: 43] cm.)

Cast off.

MAKING UP

Press as described on the information page.

Along one side of body, bring first 2 blue markers together and join row-end edge from first blue marker to red marker to cast-on edge between 2nd blue marker and red marker. In a similar way, join cast-off edge of front section between yellow and green markers to row-end edge of upper back section between yellow and green markers. Join seams along other side of body in same way. Join sleeve seams. Matching centre of sleeve cast-off edge to joined green markers and positioning sleeve seam at base of slit armhole opening, sew sleeves into armhole openings.

Front and hem band

Mark centre point of body final cast-off edge - this is back neck point. With RS facing and using 3¼mm (US 3) circular needle, beg and ending at marked centre back neck point, pick up and knit 74 [78: 88: 93: 100] sts from cast-off edge between back neck marker and yellow marker, 97 [99: 102: 104: 107] sts down left front row-end edge between yellow and blue markers, 146 [158: 176: 186: 206] sts along original cast-on edge between blue markers, 97 [99: 102: 104: 107] sts up right front row-end edge between blue and yellow markers, then 74 [78: 88: 93: 100] sts from cast-off edge between yellow marker and back neck marker. 488 [512: 556: 580: 620] sts.

Round 1 (RS): K1, P2, ★K2, P2, rep from ★ to last st, K1.

This round forms rib.

Cont in rib until band meas 8 cm from pick-up round.

Cast off **loosely** in rib.

See information page for finishing instructions.

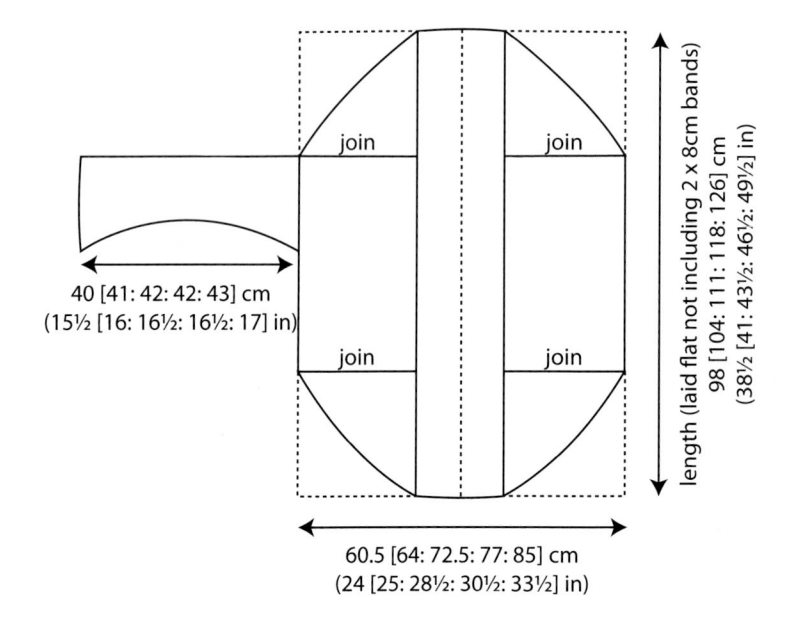

40 [41: 42: 42: 43] cm
(15½ [16: 16½: 16½: 17] in)

60.5 [64: 72.5: 77: 85] cm
(24 [25: 28½: 30½: 33½] in)

length (laid flat not including 2 x 8cm bands)
98 [104: 111: 118: 126] cm
(38½ [41: 43½: 46½: 49½] in)

Body Sizes S, XL and XXL
Sleeve Sizes S and M

18 st patt rep

86 row patt rep

key
- ☐ K on RS, P on WS
- ● P on RS
- ○ yfwd
- ╱ K2tog
- ╲ sl1, K1, psso
- △ sl1, K2tog, psso

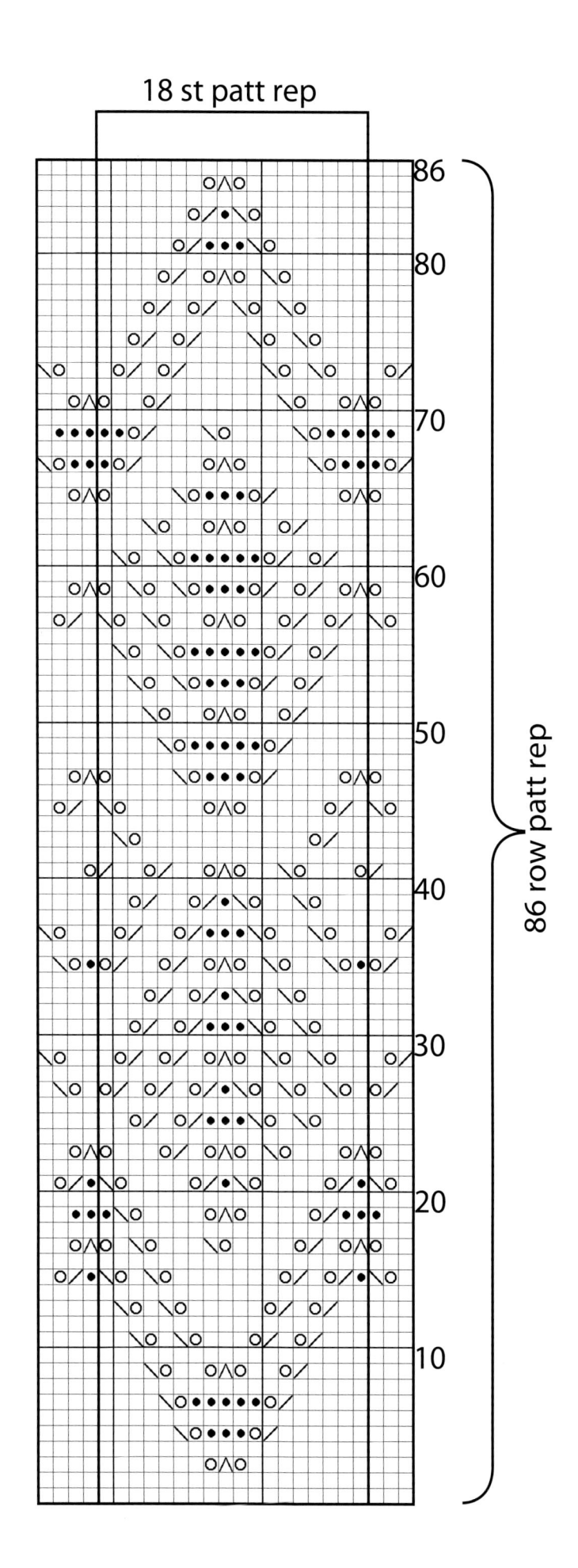

45

Body Sizes M and L
Sleeve Sizes L, XL, XXL

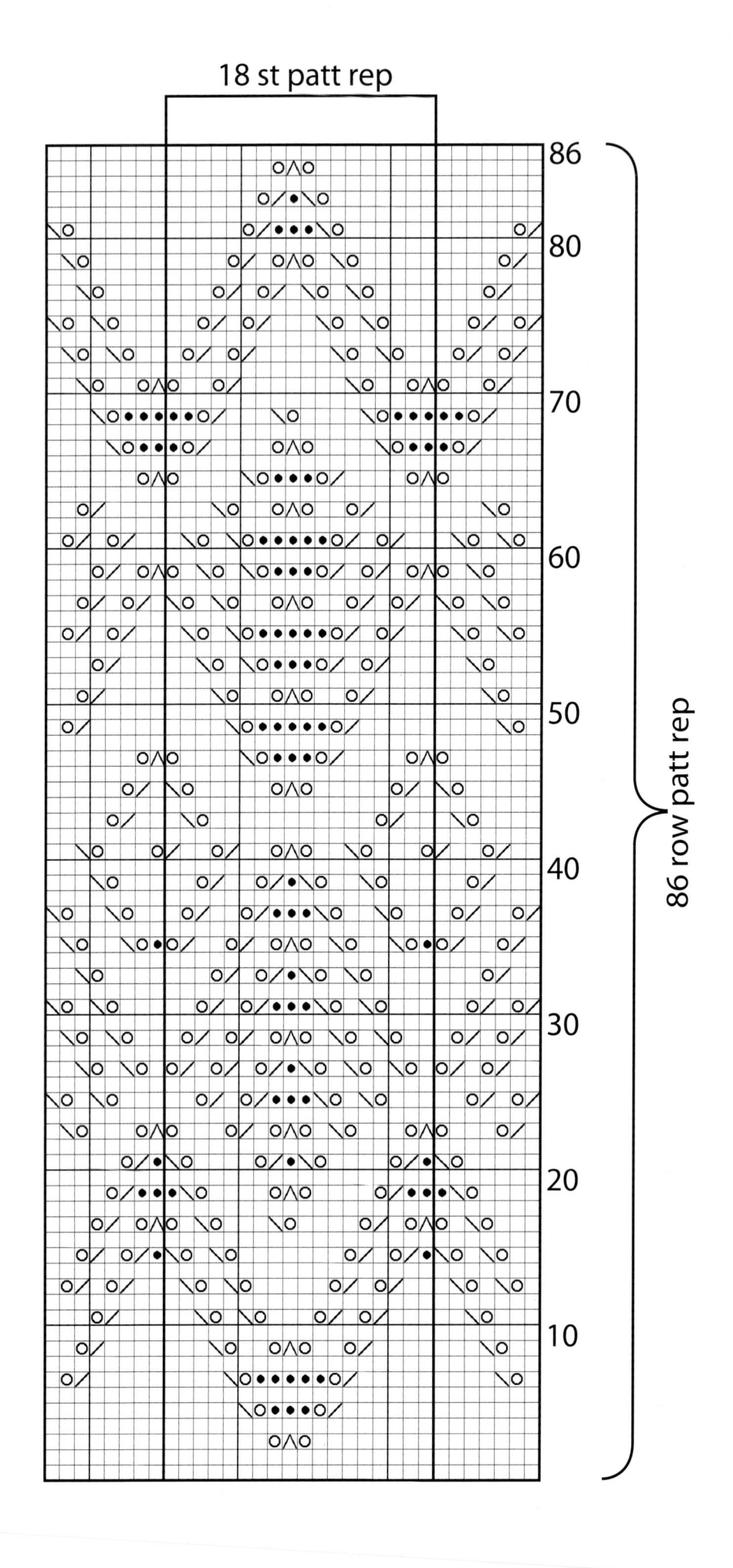

18 st patt rep

86 row patt rep

Chenin ★★

By Marie Wallin

Main Image Page 4

SIZES

S	M	L	XL	XXL	
To fit bust					
81-86	91-97	102-107	112-117	122-127	cm
32-34	36-38	40-42	44-46	48-50	in

YARN

Kidsilk Haze

6	7	8	8	9	x 25gm

(photographed in Steel 664)

NEEDLES

1 pair 2¾mm (no 12) (US 2) needles
3¼mm (no 10) (US 3) circular needle 100 cm long

BUTTONS
- 10 x BN1365 from Bedecked. Please see information page for contact details.

BEADS
- approx 800 small glass beads.

TENSION

25 sts and 34 rows to 10 cm measured over st st using 3¼mm (US 3) needles.

SPECIAL ABBREVIATION

bead 1 = place a bead by taking yarn to RS of work and slipping bead up next to st just worked, slip next st purlwise from left needle to right needle and bring yarn back to WS of work, leaving bead sitting in front of slipped st on RS.

Beading note: Before starting to knit, thread beads onto yarn. To do this, thread a fine sewing needle (one that will easily pass through the beads) with sewing thread. Knot ends of thread and then pass end of yarn through this loop. Thread a bead onto sewing thread and then gently slide it along and onto knitting yarn. Continue in this way until required number of beads are on yarn.

BODY (worked in one piece)
Using 3¼mm (US 3) circular needle cast on 752 [768: 784: 800: 816] sts.
Counting in from one end of cast-on edge, place marker after 4th st, (miss next 93 [95: 97: 99: 101] sts and place another marker) 8 times - there should be 4 sts left after 9th marker.
Beg with a K row, work in st st as folls:

Size XXL only
Work 4 rows.
Next row (RS): K4, (slip marker onto right needle, K2tog, K to within 2 sts of next marker, sl 1, K1, psso) 8 times, slip 9th marker onto right needle, K4. 800 sts.

Sizes XL and XXL only
Work - [-: -: 4: 3] rows.
Next row (RS): K4, (slip marker onto right needle, K2tog, K to within 2 sts of next marker, sl 1, K1, psso) 8 times, slip 9th marker onto right needle, K4. 784 sts.

Sizes L, XL and XXL only
Work - [-: 4: 3: 3] rows.
Next row (RS): K4, (slip marker onto right needle, K2tog, K to within 2 sts of next marker, sl 1, K1, psso) 8 times, slip 9th marker onto right needle, K4. 768 sts.

Sizes M, L, XL and XXL only
Work - [2: 1: 1: 1] rows.
Next row (RS): K4, (slip marker onto right needle, K2tog, K to within 2 sts of next marker, sl 1, K1, psso) 8 times, slip 9th marker onto right needle, K4. 752 sts.

All sizes
Work 4 [3: 3: 3: 3] rows.
Now work in shaping patt as folls:
Row 1 (RS): K2, K2tog tbl, yfwd (to make first buttonhole), (slip marker onto right needle, K2tog, K to within 2 sts of next marker, sl 1, K1, psso) 8 times, slip 9th marker onto right needle, K4. 736 sts.
Working a further 5 buttonholes in this way on every foll 24th row and noting that no further reference will be made to buttonholes,

cont as folls:
Work 3 rows.
Row 5: K4, (slip marker onto right needle, K2tog, K to within 2 sts of next marker, sl 1, K1, psso) 8 times, slip 9th marker onto right needle, K4. 720 sts.
Work 3 rows.
Row 9: As row 5. 704 sts.
Work 1 row.
Row 11: As row 5. 688 sts.
Work 3 rows.
Last 14 rows form shaping patt – 16 sts decreased on every dec row (one st at each side of the 8 sections between markers) and 4 dec rows worked for every 14 rows knitted.
Work in shaping patt for a further 20 rows, ending after patt row 6 and with RS facing for next row. 592 sts.

Place left sleeve motif
Next row (RS): K to within 13 sts of 7th marker, work next 43 sts as row 1 of motif chart, K to end.
Next row: P to within 30 sts of 3rd marker (this was 7th marker on previous row), work next 43 sts as row 2 of motif chart, P to end.
These 2 rows set position of motif chart.
Keeping motif chart correct as now set until all 34 rows have been completed and then working sts above motif chart in st st, cont as folls:
Work in shaping patt for 58 rows, ending with RS facing for next row. 320 sts.
Now place neck chart as folls:
Next row (RS): K4, (work next 39 sts as row 1 of neck chart) 8 times, K4. 304 sts.
Next row: P4, (work next 37 sts as row 2 of neck chart) 8 times, P4.
These 2 rows set the sts – neck chart between each pair of markers and first and last sts still in st st.
Working shaping as set on chart, cont from chart until all 30 rows have been completed, ending with RS facing for next row. 176 sts.
Cast off **firmly** (as this cast-off edge will support weight of garment).
Remove all markers. Now place new markers around cast-on edge as folls: place a blue marker after 57th [63rd: 70th: 78th: 87th] cast-on st, ★miss next 103 [100: 95: 91: 85] sts and then place a red marker, miss next 60 [62: 66: 66: 68] sts and place another red marker, miss next 103 [100: 95: 91: 85] sts★, place green marker, miss next 106 [118: 132: 148: 166] sts and place 2nd green marker, rep from ★ to ★ once more, place another blue marker – there should be 57 [63: 70: 78: 87] sts after this last marker.

CUFFS (both alike)
With RS facing and using 2¾mm (US 2) needles, pick up and knit 59 [61: 65: 65: 67] sts between pair of red markers (this is one st less than between markers).

Row 1 (WS): P1, ★K1, P1, rep from ★ to end.
Row 2: K1, ★P1, K1, rep from ★ to end.
These 2 rows form rib.
Cont in rib, dec 1 st at each end of 4th and 1 [1: 5: 5: 5] foll 6th rows, then on 5 [5: 2: 2: 2] foll 8th rows. 45 [47: 49: 49: 51] sts.
Work 7 rows, ending with RS facing for next row.
Cast off in rib.

BACK HEM BORDER
With RS facing and using 2¾mm (US 2) needles, pick up and knit 105 [117: 131: 147: 165] sts between pair of green markers (this is one st less than between markers).
Beg with row 1, work in rib as given for cuffs for 51 rows, ending with RS facing for next row.
Cast off in rib.

LEFT FRONT HEM BORDER
With RS facing and using 2¾mm (US 2) needles, pick up and knit 56 [62: 70: 78: 86] sts between left front opening edge and blue marker (this is 1 [1: 0: 0: 1] st less than between marker and row-end edge).
Row 1 (WS): ★P1, K1, rep from ★ to end.
Row 2: K2, ★P1, K1, rep from ★ to end.
These 2 rows form rib.
Cont in rib for a further 49 rows, ending with RS facing for next row.
Cast off in rib.

RIGHT FRONT HEM BORDER
With RS facing and using 2¾mm (US 2) needles, pick up and knit 56 [62: 70: 78: 86] sts between blue marker and right front opening edge (this is 1 [1: 0: 0: 1] st less than between marker and row-end edge).
Row 1 (WS): ★K1, P1, rep from ★ to end.
Row 2: ★K1, P1, rep from ★ to last 2 sts, K2.
These 2 rows form rib.
Work in rib for a further 3 rows, ending with RS facing for next row.
Row 6 (RS): Rib to last 4 sts, yrn, P2tog (to make a buttonhole), rib 2.
Work 13 rows.
Rep last 14 rows twice more, then row 6 again – 4 buttonholes made.
Work a further 3 rows, ending with RS facing for next row.
Cast off in rib.

MAKING UP
Press as described on the information page.
Join side and sleeve seams using back stitch, or mattress stitch if preferred, from cast-off edge of cuffs to cast-off edge of hem borders.

Neckband

With RS facing and using 2¾mm (US 2) needles, beg and ending at front opening edges, pick up and knit 176 sts from cast-off edge of body.

Beg with a P row, work in st st for 4 rows, ending with **WS** facing for next row.

Cast off purlwise (on **WS**).

Left front facing

Using 2¾mm (US 2) needles cast on 7 sts.

Row 1 (RS): K2, P1, K1, P1, K2.
Row 2: K1, (P1, K1) 3 times.
These 2 rows form rib.

Cont in rib until facing fits up entire left front opening edge, from cast-off edge of hem border to pick-up row of neckband, ending with RS facing for next row.

Cast off in rib.

Right front facing

Work as given for left front facing with the addition of 10 buttonholes worked to correspond with buttonholes along right front opening edge as folls:

Buttonhole row (RS): K2, P1, yrn, P2tog (to make a buttonhole), K2.

Slip facings to front opening edges, then fold facings to inside and neatly sew in place.

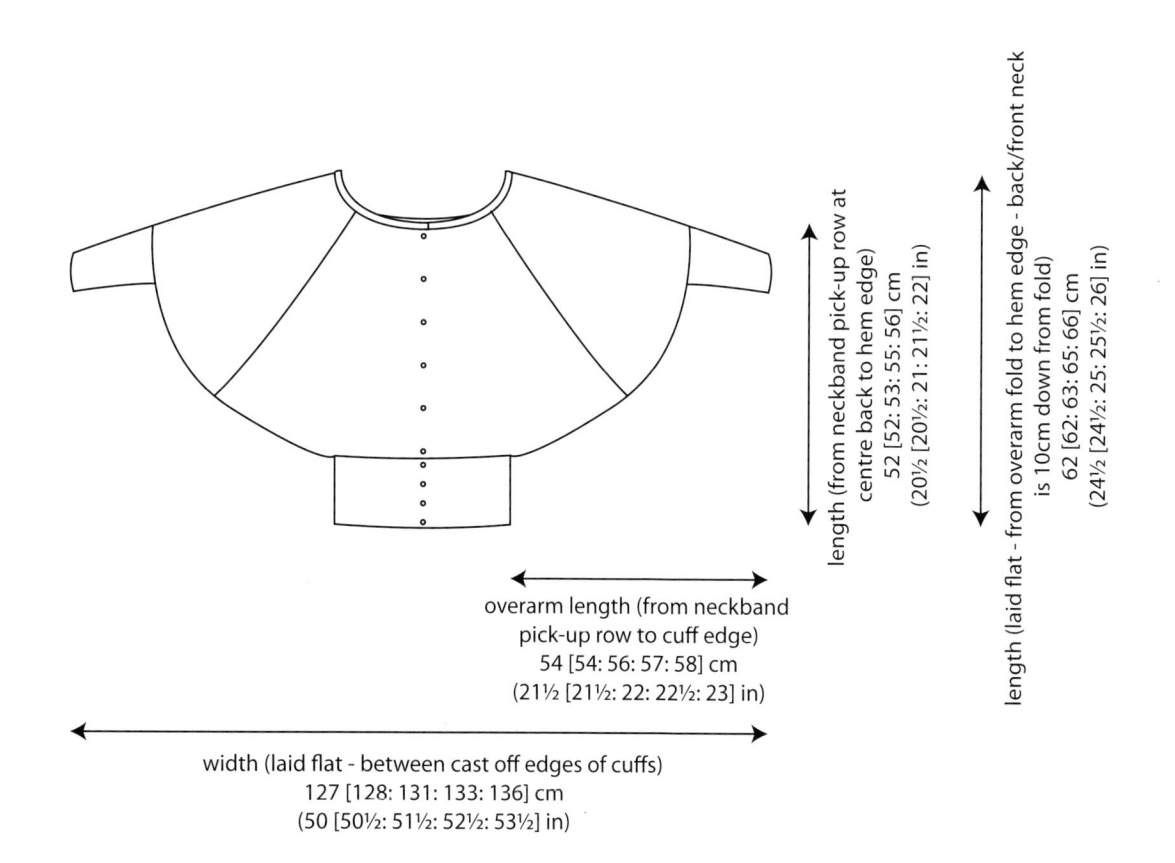

length (from neckband pick-up row at centre back to hem edge)
52 [52: 53: 55: 56] cm
(20½ [20½: 21: 21½: 22] in)

length (laid flat - from overarm fold to hem edge - back/front neck is 10cm down from fold)
62 [62: 63: 65: 66] cm
(24½ [24½: 25: 25½: 26] in)

overarm length (from neckband pick-up row to cuff edge)
54 [54: 56: 57: 58] cm
(21½ [21½: 22: 22½: 23] in)

width (laid flat - between cast off edges of cuffs)
127 [128: 131: 133: 136] cm
(50 [50½: 51½: 52½: 53½] in)

Neck Chart

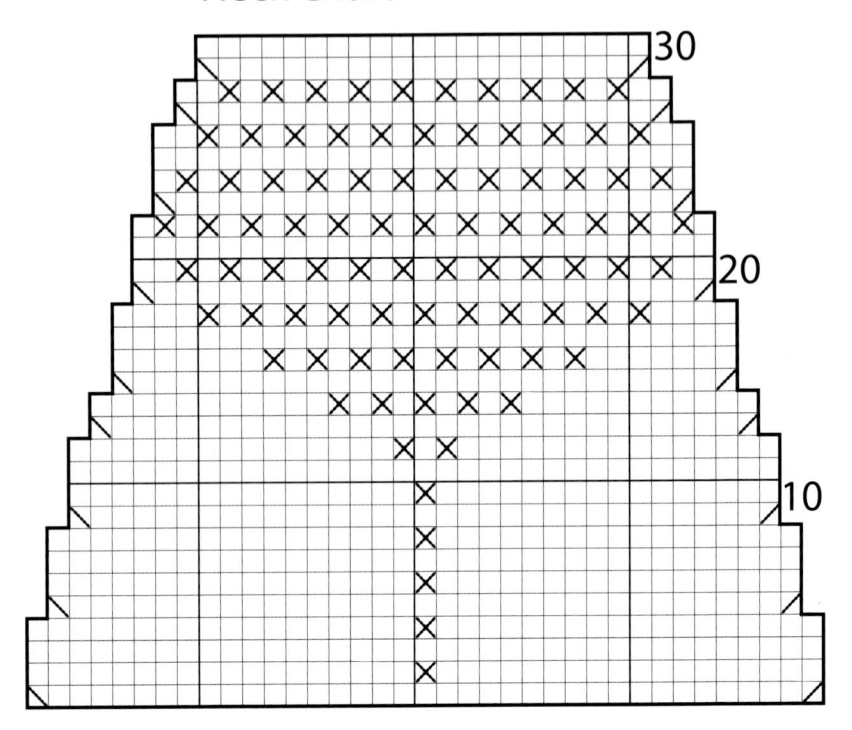

Motif Chart

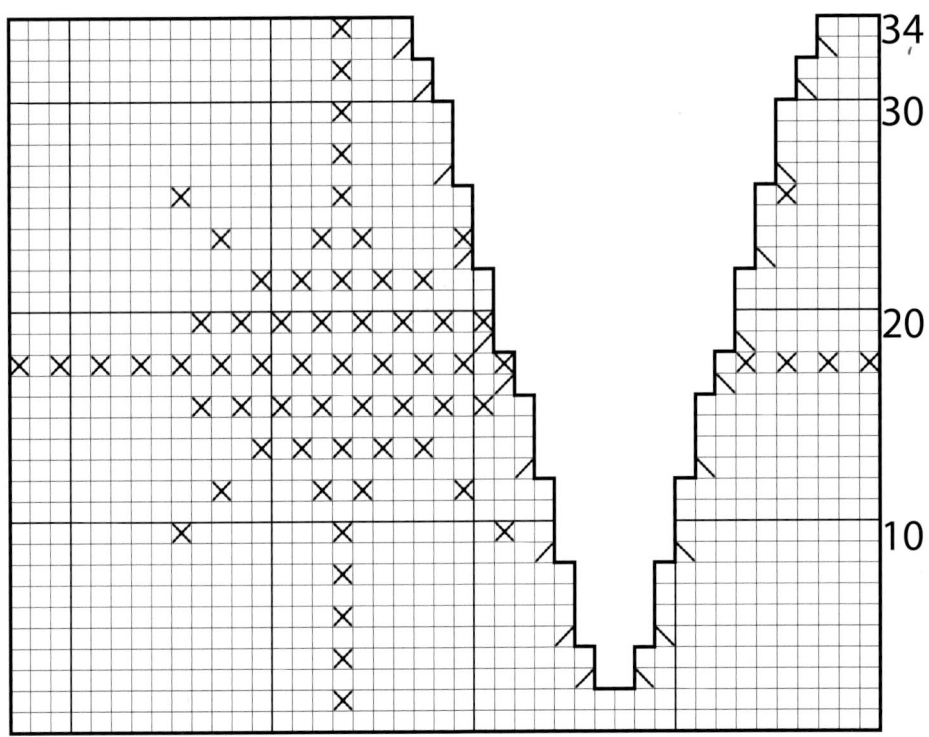

key
- ☐ K on RS, P on WS
- ☒ bead 1
- ◪ K2tog
- ◨ sl1, K1, psso

Merlot **
By Marie Wallin

Main Image Page 25

SIZES

S	M	L	XL	XXL	
To fit bust					
81-86	91-97	102-107	112-117	122-127	cm
32-34	36-38	40-42	44-46	48-50	in

YARN

Kidsilk Haze and Anchor Artiste Metallic

A Kidsilk Haze Majestic 589

4	4	4	5	5	x 25gm

B Metallic Mid Grey 324

7	8	8	8	9	x 25gm

NEEDLES

1 pair 3¼mm (no 10) (US 3) needles
2¾mm (no 12) (US 2) circular needle, one 40 cm long and one 80 cm long

TENSION

26 sts and 32 rows to 10 cm measured over patt using 3¼mm (US 3) needles.

SPECIAL ABBREVIATION

MB = make bobble as folls: (K1, P1, K1, P1, K1) all into next st, (turn and P5, turn and K5) twice, lift 2nd, 3rd, 4th and 5th sts on right needle over first st and off right needle.

BACK

Using 3¼mm (US 3) needles and one strand each of yarns A and B held together cast on 75 [81: 89: 97: 105] sts.
Work in patt as folls:
Using one strand each of yarns A and B held together and beg with a K row, work in st st for 8 rows, ending with RS facing for next row.
Break off yarn B.
Row 9 (RS): Using yarn A, knit.
Row 10: Using yarn A, purl.
Row 11: Using yarn A, K4 [4: 2: 3: 4], MB, *K5, MB, rep from * to last 4 [4: 2: 3: 4] sts, K4 [4: 2: 3: 4].
Row 12: Using yarn A, purl.
Join in yarn B.
Using one strand each of yarns A and B held together and beg with a K row, work in st st for 8 rows, ending with RS facing for next row.
Break off yarn A.
Rows 21 to 24: As rows 9 to 12 **but using yarn B**.
These 24 rows form patt.
Cont in patt until back meas 31 [32: 33: 34: 35] cm, ending with RS facing for next row.
Cast off.

MAIN SECTION

Using 3¼mm (US 3) needles and one strand each of yarns A and B held together cast on 63 [65: 67: 71: 73] sts.
Work in patt as folls:
Using one strand each of yarns A and B held together and beg with a K row, work in st st for 4 rows, ending with RS facing for next row.
Break off yarn B.
Row 5 (RS): Using yarn A, knit.
Row 6: Using yarn A, purl.
Row 7: Using yarn A, K4 [2: 3: 2: 3], MB, *K5, MB, rep from * to last 4 [2: 3: 2: 3] sts, K4 [2: 3: 2: 3].
Row 8: Using yarn A, purl.
Join in yarn B.
Using one strand each of yarns A and B held together and beg with a K row, work in st st for 8 rows, ending with RS facing for next row.
Break off yarn A.
Rows 17 to 20: As rows 5 to 8 **but using yarn B**.
Join in yarn A.
Using one strand each of yarns A and B held together and beg with a K row, work in st st for 4 rows, ending with RS facing for next row.
These 24 rows form patt.
Cont in patt until main section meas approx 146 [158: 174: 186: 202] cm, ending after patt row 24 and with RS facing for next row.
Cast off.

MAKING UP

Press as described on the information page.
Join cast-on and cast-off edges of main section using back stitch, or mattress stitch if preferred, to form a loop - seam will form lower centre back seam. Along one row-end edge of loop, mark centre point of row-end edge - this is centre back neck point. Matching centre of cast-on

edge of back to seam of main section, sew cast-on edge of back to row-end edge of main section. Matching centre of cast-off edge of back to centre back neck point of main section, sew cast-off edge of back to row-end edge of main section. There should be approx 44 [48: 52: 56: 60.5] cm free along row-end edges of main section between points where back is attached.

Left armhole edging
With RS facing, using shorter 2¾mm (US 2) circular needle and one strand each of yarns A and B held together, beg at one end of cast-on edge of back, pick up and knit 114 [124: 135: 145: 157] sts along row-end edge of main section to cast-off edge of back, then 80 [83: 85: 88: 91] sts down row-end edge of back to cast-on edge.
194 [207: 220: 233: 248] sts.
Round 1: Purl.
Round 2: Knit.
Cast off **purlwise** (on RS).

Right armhole edging
With RS facing, using shorter 2¾mm (US 2) circular needle and one strand each of yarns A and B held together, beg at other end of cast-on edge of back, pick up and knit 80 [83: 85: 88: 91] sts up row-end edge of back to cast-off edge, then 114 [124: 135: 145: 157] sts along row-end edge of main section to cast-on edge of back.
194 [207: 220: 233: 248] sts.
Round 1: Purl.
Round 2: Knit.
Cast off **purlwise** (on RS).

Outer edging
With RS facing, using longer 2¾mm (US 2) circular needle and one strand each of yarns A and B held together, beg and ending at lower edge of centre back seam, pick up and knit 379 [410: 452: 483: 525] sts evenly along entire row-end edge of main section.
Round 1: Purl.
Round 2: Knit.
Cast off **purlwise** (on RS).
See information page for finishing instructions.

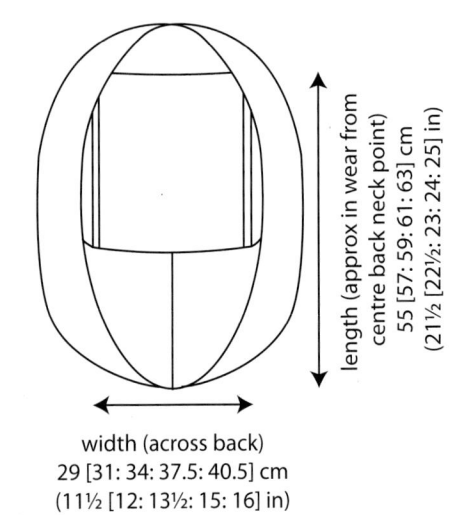

length (approx in wear from centre back neck point)
55 [57: 59: 61: 63] cm
(21½ [22½: 23: 24: 25] in)

width (across back)
29 [31: 34: 37.5: 40.5] cm
(11½ [12: 13½: 15: 16] in)

Muscadet ★★
By Marie Wallin

Main Image Page 12

SIZES

S	M	L	XL	XXL	
To fit bust					
81-86	91-97	102-107	112-117	122-127	cm
32-34	36-38	40-42	44-46	48-50	in

YARN
Kidsilk Haze and Anchor Artiste Metallic

A Kidsilk Haze Brick 649					
3	3	3	4	4	x 25gm
A Metallic Bronze 314					
3	3	3	4	4	x 25gm
B Kidsilk Haze Ember 644					
3	3	3	4	4	x 25gm
B Metallic Gold 300					
2	2	2	2	2	x 25gm
C Kidsilk Haze Ghost 642					
3	3	3	3	3	x 25gm
C Metallic Silver 301					
2	2	2	2	2	x 25gm
D Kidsilk Haze Majestic 589					
10	11	12	13	15	x 25gm
D Metallic Mid Grey 324					
9	10	11	13	14	x 25gm

NEEDLES
1 pair 2¾mm (no 12) (US 2) needles
1 pair 3¼mm (no 10) (US 3) needles
3.00mm (no 11) (US C2) crochet hook

TENSION
Body: 26 sts and 32 rows to 10 cm measured over st st using 3¼mm (US 3) needles and one strand each of Kidsilk Haze and Artiste Metallic held together.
Sleeves: 23 sts to 10 cm and one patt rep (16 rows) to **9.5** cm measured over patt using 3.00mm (US C2) crochet hook and one strand each of Kidsilk Haze and Artiste Metallic held together.

CROCHET ABBREVIATIONS
ch = chain; **dc** = double crochet; **dc2tog** = (insert hook as indicated, yoh and draw loop through) twice, yoh and draw through all 3 loops on hook; **dtr** = double treble; **dtr2tog** = ★(yoh) twice and insert hook as indicated, yoh and draw loop through, (yoh and draw through 2 loops) twice, rep from ★ once more, yoh and draw through all 3 loops; **qtr** = quadruple treble; **sp(s)** = space(s); **ss** = slip stitch; **tr** = treble; **ttr** = triple treble; **ttr2tog** = ★(yoh) 3 times and insert hook as indicated, yoh and draw loop through, (yoh and draw through 2 loops) 3 times, rep from ★ once more, yoh and draw through all 3 loops; **ttr4tog** = ★(yoh) 3 times and insert hook as indicated, yoh and draw loop through, (yoh and draw through 2 loops) 3 times, rep from ★ 3 times more, yoh and draw through all 5 loops; **yoh** = yarn over hook.

Pattern note: Garment is made using 2 strands of yarn held together throughout - one strand of Kidsilk Haze and corresponding colour strand of Artiste Metallic. Where each yarn "colour" is given in instructions, refer to yarn section (above) for which colours to use together. (For example, yarn A is one strand of Kidsilk Haze in Brick 649 and one strand of Artiste Metallic in Bronze 314 held together.)

BACK
Using 2¾mm (US 2) needles and yarn D (see pattern note) cast on 109 [123: 137: 153: 171] sts.
Row 1 (RS): K1, ★P1, K1, rep from ★ to end.
Row 2: P1, ★K1, P1, rep from ★ to end.
These 2 rows form rib.
Work in rib for a further 4 rows, ending with RS facing for next row.
Change to 3¼mm (US 3) needles.
Beg with a K row, work in st st, shaping side seams by dec 1 st at each end of 5th and 4 foll 6th rows. 99 [113: 127: 143: 161] sts.
Work 23 rows, ending with RS facing for next row.
Inc 1 st at each end of next and 4 foll 10th rows.
109 [123: 137: 153: 171] sts.
Cont straight until back meas 35 [36: 37: 38: 39] cm, ending with RS facing for next row.
Shape armholes
Cast off 5 [6: 7: 8: 9] sts at beg of next 2 rows.

99 [111: 123: 137: 153] sts.★★

Dec 1 st at each end of next 3 [5: 7: 7: 9] rows, then on foll 5 [6: 6: 9: 11] alt rows. 83 [89: 97: 105: 113] sts.

Cont straight until armhole meas 17 [18: 19: 20: 21] cm, ending with RS facing for next row.

Shape back neck

Next row (RS): K15 [18: 21: 25: 28] and turn, leaving rem sts on a holder.

Work each side of neck separately.

Dec 1 st at neck edge of next row, ending with RS facing for next row. 14 [17: 20: 24: 27] sts.

Shape shoulder

Dec 1 st at neck edge of next 4 rows, ending with RS facing for next row, **and at same time** cast off 3 [4: 5: 7: 8] sts at beg of next and foll alt row.

Cast off rem 4 [5: 6: 6: 7] sts.

With RS facing, rejoin yarn to rem sts, cast off centre 53 [53: 55: 55: 57] sts, K to end.

Complete to match first side, reversing shapings.

FRONT

Work as given for back to ★★.

Dec 1 st at each end of next 3 [5: 7: 7: 9] rows, then on foll 4 [4: 3: 5: 4] alt rows. 85 [93: 103: 113: 127] sts.

Work 1 row, ending with RS facing for next row.

Shape front neck

Next row (RS): K2tog, K26 [30: 34: 39: 45] and turn, leaving rem sts on a holder.

Work each side of neck separately.

Dec 1 st at neck edge of next 10 rows, then on foll 4 alt rows, then on 2 foll 4th rows, then on foll 6th row **and at same time** dec 1 st at armhole edge of 0 [2nd: 2nd: 2nd: 2nd] and foll 0 [0: 1: 2: 5] alt rows. 10 [13: 16: 20: 23] sts.

Cont straight until front matches back to beg of shoulder shaping, ending with RS facing for next row.

Shape shoulder

Cast off 3 [4: 5: 7: 8] sts at beg of next and foll alt row.

Work 1 row.

Cast off rem 4 [5: 6: 6: 7] sts.

With RS facing, rejoin yarn to rem sts, cast off centre 29 [29: 31: 31: 33] sts, K to last 2 sts, K2tog.

Complete to match first side, reversing shapings.

SLEEVE STRIPE SEQUENCE

Row 1 (RS): Using yarn B.
Rows 2 and 3: Using yarn C.
Row 4: Using yarn D.
Rows 5 and 6: Using yarn B.
Row 7: Using yarn A.
Rows 8 and 9: Using yarn C.
Rows 10 and 11: Using yarn D.
Row 12: Using yarn A.
Rows 13 and 14: Using yarn B.
Rows 15 and 16: Using yarn D.

These 16 rows form stripe sequence and are repeated.

SLEEVES

Using 3.00mm (US C2) crochet hook and yarn A, make 98 [100: 102: 102: 102] ch.

Row 1 (WS): 1 dc into 2nd ch from hook, 1 dc into each ch to end, turn. 97 [99: 101: 101: 101] sts.

Row 2: 1 ch (does NOT count as st), 1 dc into each dc to end, turn.

Row 3: As row 2.

Joining in and breaking off colours as required and beg with stripe row 1, cont in stripe sequence (see above) in patt as folls:

Size S only

Row 4: 4 ch (counts as 1 tr and 1 ch), miss first 2 dc, 1 tr into next dc, (1 ch, miss 1 dc, 1 tr into next dc) 4 times, (1 ch, miss 1 dc, 1 dc into next dc) twice, 1 ss into each of next 4 dc, turn, leaving rem 78 sts unworked.

Row 5: 1 ch (does NOT count as st), 1 dc into each of first 4 ss, 1 dc into each dc, ch sp or tr to end, working last dc into 3rd of 4 ch at beg of round, turn.

Row 6: 1 ch (does NOT count as st), 2 dc into first dc, 1 dc into each of next 22 sts, 1 ss into each of next 19 sts, turn, leaving rem 55 sts unworked.

Row 7: 1 ch (does NOT count as st), 1 dc into each of first 2 ss, 3 ch, miss 3 ss, 1 tr into each of next 3 ss, 3 ch, miss 3 ss, 1 dtr into each of next 3 ss, 3 ch, miss 3 ss, 1 ttr into each of next 3 sts, (3 ch, miss 3 dc, 1 ttr into each of next 3 dc) 3 times, 3 ch, miss 3 dc, 1 ttr into next dc, (2 ttr, 2 ch and 1 ttr) into last dc, turn.

Row 8: 1 ch (does NOT count as st), 2 dc into first ttr, 2 dc into first ch sp, (1 dc into each of next 3 sts, 3 dc into next ch sp) 7 times, 1 dc into each of next 7 dc, 1 ss into each of next 5 dc, turn, leaving rem 45 sts unworked.

Row 9: 1 ch (does NOT count as st), 1 dc into each st to last dc, 2 dc into last dc, turn.

Row 10: 3 ch (counts as 1 tr), 1 tr into st at base of 3 ch, 1 ch, 1 tr into next dc, (1 ch, miss 1 dc, 1 tr into next dc) 31 times, (1 ch, miss 1 dc, 1 dc into next dc) twice, 1 ch, miss 1 dc, 1 ss into each of next 5 dc, turn, leaving rem 30 sts unworked.

Row 11: 1 ch (does NOT count as st), 1 dc into each ss, ch sp, dc or tr to 3 ch at beg of previous row, 2 dc into top of 3 ch, turn.

Row 12: 1 ch (does NOT count as st), 2 dc into first dc, 1 dc into each of next 81 dc, 1 ss into each of next 5 dc, turn, leaving rem 20 sts unworked.

Row 13: 1 ch (does NOT count as st), 1 dc into each ss or dc to last st, 2 dc into last dc, turn.

Row 14: 1 ch (does NOT count as st), 2 dc into first dc, 1 dc into each of next 93 dc, 1 ss into each of last 15 dc, turn.

Row 15: 3 ch (counts as 1 tr), miss ss at base of 3 ch, 1 tr into each of next 2 ss, 3 ch, miss 3 ss, 1 dtr into each of next 3 ss, 3 ch, miss 3 ss, 1 ttr into each of next 3 ss, (3 ch, miss 3 dc, 1 ttr into each of next 3 dc) 15 times, 3 ch, miss 3 dc, 1 ttr into next dc, (2 ttr, 2 ch and 1 ttr) into last dc, turn. 114 sts.

Row 16: 1 ch (does NOT count as st), 2 dc into first ttr, 2 dc into next ch sp, (1 dc into each of next 3 sts, 3 dc into next ch sp) 18 times, 1 dc into each of next 2 tr, 1 dc into top of 3 ch at beg of previous row, turn. 115 sts.

Row 17: 1 ch (does NOT count as st), 1 dc into each dc to last dc, 2 dc into last dc, turn.

Row 18: 1 ch (does NOT count as st), 2 dc into first dc, 1 dc into each dc to end, turn.

Row 19: As row 17. 118 sts.

Row 20: 3 ch (counts as first tr), 1 tr into st at base of 3 ch, 1 ch, 1 tr into next dc, *1 ch, miss 1 dc, 1 tr into next dc, rep from * to end, turn.

Row 21: 1 ch (does NOT count as st), 1 dc into first tr, *1 dc into next ch sp, 1 dc into next tr, rep from * to last st, 2 dc into top of 3 ch at beg of previous row, turn. 121 sts.

Row 22: 1 ch (does NOT count as st), 1 dc into each dc to end, turn.

Row 23: 5 ch (counts as first ttr), miss dc at base of 5 ch, 1 ttr into each of next 2 dc, *3 ch, miss 3 dc, 1 ttr into each of next 3 dc, rep from * to last 4 sts, 3 ch, miss 3 dc, 3 ttr into last dc, turn.

Row 24: 1 ch (does NOT count as st), 1 dc into first ttr, 3 dc into next ch sp, *1 dc into each of next 3 ttr, 3 dc into next ch sp, rep from * to last 3 sts, 1 dc into each of next 2 ttr, 1 dc into top of 5 ch at beg of previous row, turn.

Row 25: 1 ch (does NOT count as st), 1 dc into each dc to end, turn.

Row 26: 4 ch (counts as 1 tr and 1 ch), miss first 2 dc, 1 tr into next dc, *1 ch, miss 1 dc, 1 tr into next dc, rep from * to end, turn.

Row 27: 1 ch (does NOT count as st), 1 dc into first tr, *1 dc into next ch sp, 1 dc into next tr, rep from * to end, working dc at end of last rep into 3rd of 4 ch at beg of previous row, turn.

Rows 28 to 30: As row 25.

Rows 31 and 32: As rows 23 and 24.

Rows 33 to 35: As row 25.

Row 36: 3 ch (counts as first tr), miss first 2 dc, 1 tr into next dc, *1 ch, miss 1 dc, 1 tr into next dc, rep from * to end, turn.

Row 37: 1 ch (does NOT count as st), 1 dc into each ch sp and tr to last 2 sts, dc2tog over last 2 sts (this is 3 ch at beg of previous row and first tr worked at beg of previous row), turn.

Row 38: 1 ch (does NOT count as st), dc2tog over first 2 sts, 1 dc into each dc to end, turn.

Row 39: 5 ch (counts as first ttr), miss dc at base of 5 ch, 1 ttr into each of next 2 dc, *3 ch, miss 3 dc, 1 ttr into each of next 4 dc, rep from * to last 7 sts, 2 ch, miss 3 dc, ttr4tog over last 4 sts, turn.

Row 40: 1 ch (does NOT count as st), miss ttr4tog at base of 1 ch, 2 dc into first ch sp, *1 dc into each of next 3 ttr**, 3 dc into next ch sp, rep from * to end, ending last rep at ** with a dc into top of 5 ch at beg of previous row, turn. 113 sts.

Row 41: Ss across and into 6th dc, 1 ch (does NOT count as st), 1 dc into same place as last ss, 1 dc into each dc to last 2 dc, dc2tog over last 2 dc, turn.

Row 42: 3 ch (does NOT count as st), miss dc2tog at base of 3 ch, 1 tr into next dc, miss 1 dc, 1 tr into next dc, (1 ch, miss 1 dc, 1 tr into next dc) 46 times, (1 ch, miss 1 dc, 1 dc into next dc) 3 times, turn, leaving rem 10 sts unworked.

Row 43: Ss across and into 11th st, 1 ch (does NOT count as st), 1 dc into tr at base of 1 ch, (1 dc into next ch sp, 1 dc into next tr) 43 times, 1 dc into last ch sp, dc2tog over next 2 tr, turn.

Row 44: 1 ch (does NOT count as st), dc2tog over first 2 sts, 1 dc into each of next 82 dc, turn, leaving rem 25 sts unworked.

Row 45: Ss across and into 6th st, 1 ch (does NOT count as st), 1 dc into dc at base of 1 ch, 1 dc into each dc to last 2 sts, dc2tog over last 2 sts, turn.

Row 46: 1 ch (does NOT count as st), dc2tog over first 2 sts, 1 dc into each of next 70 dc, turn, leaving rem 35 sts unworked.

Row 47: Ss across and into 6th st, 1 ch (does NOT count as st), 1 dc into st at base of 1 ch, 1 ch, miss 1 dc, 1 dc into each of next 3 dc, 3 ch, miss 3 dc, 1 tr into each of next 2 dc, 1 dtr into next dc, 3 ch, miss 3 dc, 1 dtr into next dc, 1 ttr into each of next 2 dc, (3 ch, miss 3 dc, 1 ttr into each of next 3 dc) 7 times, 2 ch, miss 3 dc, ttr4tog over last 4 sts, turn.

Row 48: 1 ch (does NOT count as st), miss ttr4tog at end of previous row, 2 dc into first ch sp, (1 dc into each of next 3 ttr, 3 dc into next ch sp) 6 times, 1 dc into each of next 3 ttr, turn, leaving rem 60 sts unworked.

Row 49: Ss across and into 6th st, 1 ch (does NOT count as st), 1 dc into dc a base of 1 ch, 1 dc into each dc to last 2 dc, dc2tog over last 2 dc, turn.

Row 50: 1 ch (does NOT count as st), dc2tog over first 2 sts, 1 dc into each of next 28 dc, turn, leaving rem 70 sts unworked.

Row 51: Ss across and into 5th st, 1 ch (does NOT count as st), 1 dc into st at base of 1 ch, 1 dc into each dc to last 2 sts, dc2tog over last 2 sts, turn.

Row 52: 3 ch (does NOT count as st), miss dc2tog at base of 3 ch, 1 tr into next dc, (1 ch, miss 1 dc, 1 tr into next dc) 7 times, (1 ch, miss 1 dc, 1 dc into next dc) twice, turn, leaving rem 78 sts unworked.

Row 53: Ss across and into 9th st, 1 ch (does NOT count as st), 1 dc into st at base of 1 ch, (1 dc into next ch sp, 1 dc into next tr) 5 times, turn.

Size M only

Row 4: 4 ch (counts as 1 tr and 1 ch), miss first 2 dc, 1 tr into next dc, (1 ch, miss 1 dc, 1 tr into next dc) 4 times, (1 ch, miss 1 dc, 1 dc into next dc) twice, 1 ss into each of next 4 dc, turn, leaving rem 80 sts unworked.

Row 5: 1 ch (does NOT count as st), 1 dc into each of first 4 ss, (1 dc into next dc, 1 dc into next ch sp) twice, (1 dc into next tr, 1 dc into next ch sp) 5 times, 1 dc into 3rd of 4 ch at beg of previous row, turn.

Row 6: 1 ch (does NOT count as st), 2 dc into first dc, 1 dc into each of next 23 dc, 1 ss into each of next 20 dc, turn, leaving rem 55 sts unworked.

Row 7: 1 ch (does NOT count as st), 1 dc into each of first 2 ss, 3 ch, miss 3 ss, 1 tr into each of next 3 ss, 3 ch, miss 3 ss, 1 dtr into each of next 3 ss, 3 ch, miss 3 ss, 1 ttr into each of next 3 ss, (3 ch, miss 3 dc, 1 ttr into each of next 3 dc) 4 times, 3 ch, 2 ttr into last dc, turn.

Row 8: 1 ch (does NOT count as st), 2 dc into first ttr, 1 dc into next ttr, (3 dc into next ch sp, 1 dc into each of next 3 sts) 7 times, 3 dc into next ch sp, 1 dc into each of next 7 dc, 1 ss into each of next 5 dc, turn, leaving rem 45 sts unworked.

Row 9: 1 ch (does NOT count as st), 1 dc into each st to last dc, 2 dc into last dc, turn.

Row 10: 3 ch (counts as first tr), 1 tr into dc at base of 3 ch, 1 ch, 1 tr into next dc, (1 ch, miss 1 dc, 1 tr into next dc) 32 times, (1 ch, miss 1 dc, 1 dc into next dc) twice, 1 dc into next dc, 1 ss into each of next 5 dc, turn, leaving rem 30 sts unworked.

Row 11: 1 ch (does NOT count as st), 1 dc into each of first 5 ss, 1 dc into each of next 2 dc, (1 dc into next ch sp, 1 dc into next st) 35 times, 2 dc into 3 ch at beg of previous row, turn.

Row 12: 1 ch (does NOT count as st), 2 dc into first dc, 1 dc into each of next 83 dc, 1 ss into each of next 5 dc, turn, leaving rem 20 sts unworked.

Row 13: 1 ch (does NOT count as st), 1 dc into each of first 5 ss, 1 dc into each dc to last dc, 2 dc into last dc, turn.

Row 14: 1 ch (does NOT count as st), 2 dc into first dc, 1 dc into each of next 95 dc, 1 ss into each of last 15 dc, turn. 112 sts.

Row 15: 3 ch (counts as first tr), miss ss at base of 3 ch, 1 tr into each of next 2 ss, 3 ch, miss 3 ss, 1 dtr into each of next 3 ss, 3 ch, miss 3 ss, 1 ttr into each of next 3 ss, (3 ch, miss 3 dc, 1 ttr into each of next 3 dc) 16 times, 3 ch, 2 ttr into last dc, turn. 116 sts.

Row 16: 1 ch (does NOT count as st), 2 dc into first ttr, 1 dc into next ttr, *3 dc into next ch sp, 1 dc into each of next 3 sts, rep from * to end, working dc at end of last rep into top of 3 ch at beg of previous row.

Row 17: 1 ch (does NOT count as st), 1 dc into each dc to last dc, 2 dc into last dc, turn.

Row 18: 1 ch (does NOT count as st), 2 dc into first dc, 1 dc into each dc to end, turn.

Row 19: As row 17. 120 sts.

Row 20: 3 ch (counts as first tr), 1 tr into dc at base of 3 ch, 1 ch, 1 tr into next dc, *1 ch, miss 1 dc, 1 tr into next dc, rep from * to end, turn.

Row 21: 1 ch (does NOT count as st), 1 dc into tr at base of 1 ch, *1 dc into next ch sp, 1 dc into next tr, rep from * to last st, 2 dc into top of 3 ch at beg of previous row, turn.

Row 22: As row 18.

Row 23: 5 ch (counts as first ttr), miss dc at base of 5 ch, 1 ttr into each of next 2 dc, *3 ch, miss 3 dc, 1 ttr into each of next 3 dc, rep from * to last st, 1 ch, 1 ttr into last dc, turn.

Row 24: 1 ch (does NOT count as st), 1 dc into first ttr, 1 dc into next ch sp, *1 dc into each of next 3 ttr**, 3 dc into next ch sp, rep from * to end, ending last rep at ** by working a dc into top of 5 ch at beg of previous row, turn. 125 sts.

Row 25: 1 ch (does NOT count as st), 1 dc into each dc to end, turn.

Row 26: 4 ch (counts as 1 tr and 1 ch), miss first 2 dc, 1 tr into next dc, *1 ch, miss 1 dc, 1 tr into next dc, rep from * to end, turn.

Row 27: 1 ch (does NOT count as st), 1 dc into first tr, *1 dc into next ch sp, 1 dc into next tr, rep from * to end, working dc at end of last rep into 3rd of 4 ch at beg of previous row, turn.

Rows 28 to 30: As row 25.

Row 31: 5 ch (counts as first ttr), miss dc at base of 5 ch, 1 ttr into each of next 2 dc, *3 ch, miss 3 dc, 1 ttr into each of next 3 dc, rep from * to last 2 dc, 1 ch, miss 1 dc, 1 ttr into last dc, turn.

Row 32: As row 24.

Rows 33 to 35: As row 25.

Row 36: 3 ch (counts as first tr), miss first 2 dc, 1 tr into next dc, *1 ch, miss 1 dc, 1 tr into next dc, rep from * to end, turn.

Row 37: 1 ch (does NOT count as st), 1 dc into first tr, *1 dc into next ch sp, 1 dc into next tr, rep from * to last 3 sts, 1 dc into next ch sp, dc2tog over last 2 sts (this is 1 tr and 3 ch at beg of previous row), turn.

Row 38: 1 ch (does NOT count as st), dc2tog over first 2 sts, 1 dc into each dc to end, turn. 122 sts.

Row 39: 5 ch (counts as first ttr), miss dc at base of 5 ch, 1 ttr into each of next 2 dc, (3 ch, miss 3 dc, 1 ttr into each of next 3 dc) 19 times, miss 3 dc, ttr2tog over last 2 sts, turn.

Row 40: 1 ch (does NOT count as st), dc2tog over first 2 sts, 1 dc into each of next 2 ttr, *3 dc into next ch sp, 1 dc into each of next 3 ttr, rep from * to end, working dc at end of last rep into top of 5 ch at beg of previous row, turn.

Row 41: 1 ch (does NOT count as st), 1 dc into each dc to last 2 dc, dc2tog over last 2 dc, turn. 116 sts.

Row 42: 3 ch (does NOT count as st), miss st at base of 3 ch, 1 tr into next dc, miss 1 dc, 1 tr into next dc, *1 ch, miss 1 dc, 1 tr into next dc, rep from * to last 6 sts, (1 ch, miss 1 dc, 1 dc into next dc) 3 times, turn.

Row 43: Ss across and into 11th st, 1 ch (does NOT count as st), 1 dc into tr at base of 1 ch, (1 dc into next ch sp, 1 dc into next tr) 50 times, 1 dc into next ch sp, dc2tog over next 2 tr, turn.

Row 44: 1 ch (does NOT count as st), dc2tog over first 2 sts, 1 dc into each of next 96 dc, turn, leaving rem 15 sts unworked.

Row 45: Ss across and into 6th st, 1 ch (does NOT count as st), 1 dc into st at base of 1 ch, 1 dc into each dc to last 2 sts, dc2tog over last 2 sts, turn.

Row 46: 1 ch (does NOT count as st), dc2tog over first 2 sts, 1 dc into each of next 84 dc, turn, leaving rem 25 sts unworked.

Row 47: Ss across and into 6th st, 1 ch (does NOT count as st), 1 dc into st at base of 1 ch, 1 dc into each of next 2 dc, 3 ch, miss 3 dc, 1 dc into each of next 3 dc, 3 ch, miss 3 dc, 1 dtr into each of next 3 dc, (3 ch, miss 3 dc, 1 ttr into each of next 3 dc) 10 times, miss 3 dc, ttr2tog over last 2 dc, turn.

Row 48: 1 ch (does NOT count as st), dc2tog over first 2 sts, 1 dc into each of next 2 ttr, (3 dc into next ch sp, 1 dc into each of next 3 ttr) 8 times, 3 dc into next ch sp, 1 dc into next ttr, turn, leaving rem 50 sts unworked.

Row 49: Ss across and into 6th st, 1 ch (does NOT count as st), 1 dc into st at base of 1 ch, 1 dc into each dc to last 2 sts, dc2tog over last 2 sts, turn.

Row 50: 1 ch (does NOT count as st), dc2tog over first 2 sts, 1 dc into each of next 42 dc, turn, leaving rem 60 sts unworked.

Row 51: Ss across and into 6th st, 1 ch (does NOT count as st), 1 dc into st at base of 1 ch, 1 dc into each dc to last 2 sts, dc2tog over last 2 sts, turn.

Row 52: 3 ch (does NOT count as st), miss st at base of 3 ch, 1 tr into next dc, miss 1 dc, 1 tr into next dc, (1 ch, miss 1 dc, 1 tr into next dc) 11 times, (1 ch, miss 1 dc, 1 dc into next dc) 3 times, turn, leaving rem 70 sts unworked.

Row 53: Ss across and into 11th st, 1 ch (does NOT count as st), 1 dc into st at base of 1 ch, (1 dc into next ch sp, 1 dc into next tr) 8 times, 1 dc into next ch sp, dc2tog over last 2 tr, turn.

Row 54: 1 ch (does NOT count as st), 1 dc into each of first 15 dc, turn, leaving rem 84 sts unworked.

Row 55: Ss across and into 5th st, 1 ch (does NOT count as st), 1 dc into st at base of 1 ch, 1 ch, miss 1 dc, 1 dc into each of next 3 dc, 3 ch, miss 3 dc, 1 dc into each of next 3 dc, turn.

Size L only

Row 4: 4 ch (counts as 1 tr and 1 ch), miss first 2 dc, 1 tr into next dc, (1 ch, miss 1 dc, 1 tr into next dc) 4 times, (1 ch, miss 1 dc, 1 dc into next dc) twice, 1 ch, miss 1 dc, 1 ss into each of next 5 dc, turn, leaving rem 80 sts unworked.

Row 5: 1 ch (does NOT count as st), 1 dc into each of first 5 ss, 1 dc into each dc, ch sp or tr to end, working last dc into 3rd of 4 ch at beg of round, turn.

Row 6: 1 ch (does NOT count as st), 2 dc into first dc, 1 dc into each of next 25 sts, 1 ss into each of next 20 sts, turn, leaving rem 55 sts unworked.

Row 7: 1 ch (does NOT count as st), 1 dc into each of first 2 ss, 3 ch, miss 3 ss, 1 tr into each of next 3 ss, 3 ch, miss 3 ss, 1 dtr into each of next 3 ss, 3 ch, miss 3 ss, 1 ttr into each of next 3 ss, (3 ch, miss 3 dc, 1 ttr into each of next 3 dc) 4 times, 3 ch, miss 2 dc, 4 ttr into last dc, turn.

Row 8: 1 ch (does NOT count as st), 2 dc into first ttr, (1 dc into each of next 3 sts, 3 dc into next ch sp) 8 times, 1 dc into each of next 7 dc, 1 ss into each of next 5 dc, turn, leaving rem 45 sts unworked.

Row 9: 1 ch (does NOT count as st), 1 dc into each st to last dc, 2 dc into last dc, turn.

Row 10: 3 ch (counts as 1 tr), 1 tr into st at base of 3 ch, (1 ch, miss 1 dc, 1 tr into next dc) 34 times, (1 ch, miss 1 dc, 1 dc into next dc) twice, 1 ch, miss 1 dc, 1 ss into each of next 5 dc, turn, leaving rem 29 sts unworked.

Row 11: 1 ch (does NOT count as st), 1 dc into each ss, ch sp, dc or tr to 3 ch at beg of previous row, 2 dc into top of 3 ch, turn.

Row 12: 1 ch (does NOT count as st), 2 dc into first dc, 1 dc into each of next 85 dc, 1 ss into each of next 5 dc, turn, leaving rem 19 sts unworked.

Row 13: 1 ch (does NOT count as st), 1 dc into each ss or dc to last st, 2 dc into last dc, turn.

Row 14: 1 ch (does NOT count as st), 1 dc into each of next 97 dc, 1 ss into each of last 15 dc, turn.

Row 15: 3 ch (counts as 1 tr), miss ss at base of 3 ch, 1 tr into each of next 2 ss, 3 ch, miss 3 ss, 1 dtr into each of next 3 ss, 3 ch, miss 3 ss, 1 ttr into each of next 3 ss, (3 ch, miss 3 dc, 1 ttr into each of next 3 dc) 16 times, 3 ch, 4 ttr into last dc, turn. 118 sts.

Row 16: 1 ch (does NOT count as st), 2 dc into first ttr, (1 dc into each of next 3 sts, 3 dc into next ch sp) 19 times, 1 dc into each of next 2 tr, 1 dc into top of 3 ch at beg of previous row, turn. 119 sts.

Row 17: 1 ch (does NOT count as st), 1 dc into each dc to last dc, 2 dc into last dc, turn.

Row 18: 1 ch (does NOT count as st), 2 dc into first dc, 1 dc into each dc to end, turn.

Row 19: As row 17. 122 sts.

Row 20: 3 ch (counts as first tr), 1 tr into st at base of 3 ch, 1 ch, 1 tr into next dc, ★1 ch, miss 1 dc, 1 tr into next dc, rep from ★ to end, turn.

Row 21: 1 ch (does NOT count as st), 1 dc into first tr, ★1 dc into next ch sp, 1 dc into next tr, rep from ★ to last st, 2 dc into top of 3 ch at beg of previous row, turn.

Row 22: As row 18. 126 sts.

Row 23: 5 ch (counts as first ttr), miss dc at base of 5 ch, 1 ttr into each of next 2 dc, ★3 ch, miss 3 dc, 1 ttr into each of next 3 dc, rep from ★ to last 3 sts, 3 ch, miss 2 dc, 3 ttr into last dc, turn. 129 sts.

Row 24: 1 ch (does NOT count as st), ★1 dc into each of next 3 ttr, 3 dc into next ch sp, rep from ★ to last 3 sts, 1 dc into each of next 2 ttr, 1 dc into top of 5 ch at beg of previous row, turn.

Row 25: 1 ch (does NOT count as st), 1 dc into each dc to end, turn.

Row 26: 4 ch (counts as 1 tr and 1 ch), miss first 2 dc, 1 tr into next dc, ★1 ch, miss 1 dc, 1 tr into next dc, rep from ★ to end, turn.

Row 27: 1 ch (does NOT count as st), 1 dc into first tr, ★1 dc into next ch sp, 1 dc into next tr, rep from ★ to end, working dc at end of last rep into 3rd of 4 ch at beg of previous row, turn.

Rows 28 to 30: As row 25.

Row 31: 5 ch (counts as 1 ttr), miss dc at base of 5 ch, 1 ttr into each of next 2 dc, ★3 ch, miss 3 dc, 1 ttr into each of next 3 dc, rep from ★ to end, turn.

Row 32: As row 24.

Rows 33 to 35: As row 25.

Row 36: 3 ch (counts as first tr), miss first 2 dc, 1 tr into next tr, ★1 ch, miss 1 dc, 1 tr into next dc, rep from ★ to end, turn. 128 sts.

Row 37: 1 ch (does NOT count as st), 1 dc into first tr, ★1 dc into next ch sp, 1 dc into next tr, rep from ★ to last 3 sts, 1 dc into next ch sp, dc2tog over last 2 tr, turn. 127 sts.

Row 38: 1 ch (does NOT count as st), dc2tog over first 2 sts, 1 dc into each dc to end, turn. 126 sts.

Row 39: 5 ch (counts as first ttr), miss dc at base of 5 ch, 1 ttr into each of next 2 dc, ★3 ch, miss 3 dc, 1 ttr into each of next 3 dc, rep from ★ to last 9 sts, 3 ch, miss 3 dc, 1 ttr into next dc, ttr2tog over next 2 dc, miss 2 dc, 1 qtr into last dc, turn.

Row 40: 1 ch (does NOT count as st), miss qtr at end of previous row, dc2tog over next 2 sts, ★3 dc into next ch sp, 1 dc into each of next 3 ttr, rep from ★ to end, working dc at end of last rep into top of 5 ch at beg of previous row, turn.

Row 41: 1 ch (does NOT count as st), 1 dc into each dc to last 2 sts, dc2tog over last 2 sts, turn. 120 sts.

Row 42: 4 ch (does NOT count as st), miss st at base of 4 ch, 1 tr into next dc, miss 1 dc, 1 tr into next dc, ★1 ch, miss 1 dc, 1 tr into next dc, rep from ★ to end, turn.

Row 43: 1 ch (does NOT count as st), 1 dc into first tr, ★1 dc into next ch sp, 1 dc into next tr, rep from ★ to last 3 sts, 1 dc into next ch sp, dc2tog over next 2 tr, turn. 117 sts.

Row 44: 1 ch (does NOT count as st), dc2tog over first 2 sts, 1 dc into each dc to last 5 sts, turn, leaving rem 5 sts unworked.

Row 45: 1 ss into each of first 5 sts, 1 ch (does NOT count as st), 1 dc into each dc to last 2 sts, dc2tog over last 2 sts, turn.

Row 46: 1 ch (does NOT count as st), dc2tog over first 2 sts, 1 dc into each of next 98 dc, turn, leaving rem 15 sts unworked.

Row 47: 1 ss into each of first 5 dc, 1 ch (does NOT count as st), 1 dc into next dc, 3 ch, miss 3 dc, 1 tr into each of next 2 dc, 3 ch, miss 3 dc, 1 dtr into each of next 3 dc, (3 ch, miss 3 dc, 1 ttr into each of next 3 dc) 12 times, 3 ch, miss 3 dc, 1 ttr into next dc, ttr2tog over next 2 dc, miss 2 dc, 1 qtr into last st, turn.

Row 48: 1 ch (does NOT count as st), miss qtr at end of previous row, dc2tog over next 2 sts, (3 dc into next ch sp, 1 dc into each of next 3 ttr) 11 times, 2 dc into next ch sp, turn, leaving rem 40 sts unworked.
Row 49: 1 ss into each of first 5 dc, 1 ch (does NOT count as st), 1 dc into each dc to last 2 sts, dc2tog over last 2 sts, turn.
Row 50: 1 ch (does NOT count as st), dc2tog over first 2 sts, 1 dc into each of next 56 dc, turn, leaving rem 50 sts unworked.
Row 51: 1 ss into each of first 5 dc, 1 ch (does NOT count as st), 1 dc into each dc to last 2 sts, dc2tog over last 2 sts, turn.
Row 52: 4 ch (counts as first st), miss first 3 sts, (1 tr into next dc, 1 ch, miss 1 dc) 19 times, (1 dc into next dc, 1 ch, miss 1 dc) twice, 1 dc into next dc, turn, leaving rem 60 sts unworked.
Row 53: 1 ss into each of first 10 sts, 1 ch (does NOT count as st), (1 dc into next tr, 1 dc into next ch sp) 16 times, dc2tog over last 2 sts, turn.
Row 54: 1 ch (does NOT count as st), dc2tog over first 2 sts, 1 dc into each of next 26 dc, turn, leaving rem 75 sts unworked.
Row 55: 1 ss into each of first 5 dc, 1 ch (does NOT count as st), 1 dc into next dc, 3 ch, miss 3 dc, 1 dc into next dc, 1 tr into each of next 2 dc, 3 ch, miss 3 dc, 1 dtr into each of next 3 dc, 3 ch, miss 3 dc, 1 dtr into each of next 3 dc, 1 ch, miss 1 dc, dtr2tog over last 2 sts, turn.

Sizes XL and XXL only
Row 4: 4 ch (counts as 1 tr and 1 ch), miss first 2 dc, 1 tr into next dc, (1 ch, miss 1 dc, 1 tr into next dc) 4 times, (1 ch, miss 1 dc, 1 dc into next dc) twice, 1 ss into each of next 4 dc, turn, leaving rem 82 sts unworked.
Row 5: 1 ch (does NOT count as st), 1 dc into each of first 4 ss, (1 dc into next dc, 1 dc into next ch sp) twice, (1 dc into next tr, 1 dc into next ch sp) 5 times, 1 dc into 3rd of 4 ch at beg of previous row, turn.
Row 6: 1 ch (does NOT count as st), 2 dc into first dc, 1 dc into each of next 22 dc, 1 ss into each of next 18 dc, turn, leaving rem 60 sts unworked.
Row 7: 1 ch (does NOT count as st), 1 dc into each of first 3 ss, 3 ch, miss 3 ss, 1 tr into each of next 3 ss, 3 ch, miss 3 ss, 1 dtr into each of next 2 ss, 1 ttr into next ss, 3 ch, miss 3 ss, (1 ttr into each of next 3 dc, 3 ch, miss 3 dc) 4 times, miss 2 dc, 4 ttr into last dc, turn.
Row 8: 1 ch (does NOT count as st), 2 dc into first ttr, (1 dc into each of next 3 sts, 3 dc into next ch sp) 7 times, 1 dc into each of next 8 dc, 1 ss into each of next 5 dc, turn, leaving rem 50 sts unworked.
Row 9: 1 ch (does NOT count as st), 1 dc into each of first 5 ss, 1 dc into each of next 51 dc, 2 dc into last dc, turn.
Row 10: 3 ch (counts as 1 tr), 1 tr into st at base of 3 ch, 1 ch, 1 tr into next dc, (1 ch, miss 1 dc, 1 tr into next dc) 30 times, (1 ch, miss 1 dc, 1 dc into next dc) 3 times, 1 ss into each of next 5 dc, turn, leaving rem 35 sts unworked.
Row 11: 1 ch (does NOT count as st), 1 dc into each of first 5 ss, (1 dc into next st, 1 dc into next ch sp) 34 times, 1 dc into next tr, 2 dc into top of 3 ch at beg of previous row, turn.
Row 12: 1 ch (does NOT count as st), 2 dc into first dc, 1 dc into each of next 80 dc, 1 ss into each of next 5 dc, turn, leaving rem 25 sts unworked.
Row 13: 1 ch (does NOT count as st), 1 dc into each of first 5 ss, 1 dc into each dc to last 2 sts, 2 dc into last dc, turn.
Row 14: 1 ch (does NOT count as st), 2 dc into first dc, 1 dc into each of next 92 dc, 1 ss into each of last 20 dc, turn.
Row 15: 1 ch (does NOT count as st), 1 dc into each of first 3 ss, 3 ch, miss 3 ss, 1 tr into each of next 3 ss, 3 ch, miss 3 ss, 1 dtr into each of next 3 ss, 3 ch, miss 3 ss, 1 ttr into each of next 2 ss, 1 ttr into next dc, (3 ch, miss 3 dc, 1 ttr into each of next 3 dc) 15 times, 3 ch, miss 2 dc, 4 ttr into last dc, turn. 118 sts.
Row 16: 1 ch (does NOT count as st), 2 dc into first ttr, (1 dc into each of next 3 sts, 3 dc into next ch sp) 19 times, 1 dc into each of last 3 dc, turn.
Row 17: 1 ch (does NOT count as st), 1 dc into each dc to last dc, 2 dc into last dc, turn.
Row 18: 1 ch (does NOT count as st), 2 dc into first dc, 1 dc into each dc to end, turn.
Row 19: As row 17. 122 sts.
Row 20: 3 ch (counts as first tr), 1 tr into dc at base of 3 ch, 1 ch, 1 tr into next dc, *1 ch, miss 1 dc, 1 tr into next dc, rep from * to end, turn.
Row 21: 1 ch (does NOT count as st), 1 dc into tr a base of 1 ch, *1 dc into next ch sp, 1 dc into next tr, rep from * to last st, 2 dc into top of 3 ch at beg of previous row, turn.
Row 22: As row 18. 126 sts.
Row 23: 5 ch (counts as first ttr), miss dc at base of 5 ch, 1 ttr into each of next 2 dc, *3 ch, miss 3 dc, 1 ttr into each of next 3 dc, rep from * to last 3 sts, 3 ch, miss 2 dc, 4 ttr into next dc, turn.
Row 24: 1 ch (does NOT count as st), 2 dc into first ttr, *1 dc into each of next 3 ttr**, 3 dc into next ch sp, rep from * to end, ending last rep at ** with 1 dc into top of 5 ch at beg of previous row, turn.

Size XL only
Row 25: 1 ch (does NOT count as st), 1 dc into each dc to end, turn. 131 sts.
Row 26: 4 ch (counts as 1 tr and 1 ch), miss first 2 dc, 1 tr into next dc, *1 ch, miss 1 dc, 1 tr into next dc, rep from * to end, turn.
Row 27: 1 ch (does NOT count as st), 1 dc into tr at base of 1 ch, *1 dc into next ch sp, 1 dc into next tr, rep from * to end, working dc at end of last rep into 3rd of 4 ch at beg of previous row, turn.
Rows 28 to 30: As row 25.
Row 31: 5 ch (counts as first ttr), miss dc at base of 5 ch, 1 ttr into each of next 2 dc, *3 ch, miss 3 dc, 1 ttr into each of next 3 dc, rep from * to last 2 sts, 1 ch, miss 1 dc, 1 ttr into last dc, turn.
Row 32: 1 ch (does NOT count as st), 1 dc into first ttr, 1 dc into next ch sp, *1 dc into each of next 3 ttr**, 3 dc into next ch sp, rep from * to end, ending last rep at ** with 1 dc into top of 5 ch at beg of previous row, turn.
Rows 33 to 35: As row 25.
Row 36: 3 ch (counts as first tr), miss first 2 dc, 1 tr into next dc, *1 ch, miss 1 dc, 1 tr into next dc, rep from * to end, turn.
Row 37: 1 ch (does NOT count as st), 1 dc into tr at base of 1 ch, *1 dc into next ch sp, 1 dc into next tr, rep from * to last 3 sts, 1 dc into next ch sp, dc2tog over last 2 sts, turn.
Row 38: 1 ch (does NOT count as st), dc2tog over first 2 dc, 1 dc into each dc to end, turn. 128 sts.
Row 39: 5 ch (counts as first ttr), miss dc at base of 5 ch, 1 ttr into each of next 2 dc, *3 ch, miss 3 dc, 1 ttr into each of next 3 dc, rep from * to last 5 sts, miss 3 dc, ttr2tog over last 2 sts, turn.

Row 40: 1 ch (does NOT count as st), dc2tog over first 2 sts, 1 dc into each of next 2 ttr, *3 dc into next ch sp, 1 dc into each of next 3 ttr, rep from * to end, working dc at end of last rep into top of 5 ch at beg of previous row, turn.
Row 41: 1 ch (does NOT count as st), 1 dc into each dc to last 2 sts, dc2tog over last 2 sts, turn.
Row 42: 3 ch (does NOT count as st), miss st at base of 3 ch, 1 tr into next dc, miss 1 dc, 1 tr into next dc, *1 ch, miss 1 dc, 1 tr into next dc, rep from * to end, turn.
Row 43: 1 ch (does NOT count as st), 1 dc into first tr, *1 dc into next ch sp, 1 dc into next tr, rep from * to last 3 sts, 1 dc into next ch sp, dc2tog over last 2 sts, turn.
Row 44: 1 ch (does NOT count as st), dc2tog over first 2 sts, 1 dc into each dc to end, turn. 118 sts.
Row 45: Ss across and into 6th st, 1 ch (does NOT count as st), 1 dc into same place as last ss, 1 dc into each dc to last 2 sts, dc2tog over last 2 sts, turn.
Row 46: 1 ch (does NOT count as st), dc2tog over first 2 sts, 1 dc into each of next 105 dc, turn, leaving rem 10 sts unworked.
Row 47: Ss across and into 6th st, 1 ch (does NOT count as st), 1 dc into same place as last ss, 2 ch, miss 2 dc, 1 dc into each of next 2 dc, 1 tr into next dc, 3 ch, miss 3 dc, 1 tr into next dc, 1 dtr into each of next 2 dc, (3 ch, miss 3 dc, 1 ttr into each of next 3 dc) 14 times, miss 3 dc, ttr2tog over last 2 sts, turn.
Row 48: 1 ch (does NOT count as st), dc2tog over first 2 sts, 1 dc into each of next 2 ttr, (3 dc into next ch sp, 1 dc into each of next 3 ttr) 12 times, 1 dc into next ch sp, turn, leaving rem 35 sts unworked.
Row 49: Ss across and into 6th st, 1 ch (does NOT count as st), 1 dc into same place as last ss, 1 dc into each dc to last 2 sts, dc2tog over last 2 sts, turn.
Row 50: 1 ch (does NOT count as st), dc2tog over first 2 sts, 1 dc into each of next 63 dc, turn, leaving rem 45 sts unworked.
Row 51: Ss across and into 6th st, 1 ch (does NOT count as st), 1 dc into same place as last ss, 1 dc into each dc to last 2 sts, dc2tog over last 2 sts, turn.
Row 52: 3 ch (does NOT count as st), miss st at base of 3 ch, 1 tr into next dc, miss 1 dc, 1 tr into next dc, (1 ch, miss 1 dc, 1 tr into next dc) 22 times, (1 ch, miss 1 dc, 1 dc into next dc) twice, 1 dc into next dc, turn, leaving rem 55 sts unworked.
Row 53: Ss across and into 11th st, 1 ch (does NOT count as st), 1 dc into ch sp at base of 1 ch, *1 dc into next tr, 1 dc into next ch sp, rep from * to last 2 tr, dc2tog over last 2 tr, turn.
Row 54: 1 ch (does NOT count as st), dc2tog over first 2 sts, 1 dc into each of next 33 dc, turn, leaving rem 70 sts unworked.
Row 55: Ss across and into 5th st, 1 ch (does NOT count as st), 1 dc into same place as last ss, 3 ch, miss 3 dc, 1 tr into each of next 3 dc, 3 ch, miss 3 dc, 1 dtr into each of next 2 dc, 1 ttr into next dc, (3 ch, miss 3 dc, 1 ttr into each of next 3 dc) twice, 1 ch, miss 3 dc, ttr2tog over last 2 sts, turn.
Row 56: 1 ch (does NOT count as st), 1 dc into each of first 11 sts. Fasten off.
Rejoin yarn at beg of row 56.
Size XXL only

Row 25: 1 ch (does NOT count as st), 1 dc into each dc to last dc, 2 dc into last dc, turn.
Row 26: 4 ch (counts as 1 tr and 1 ch), miss dc at base of 4 ch, 1 tr into next dc, *1 ch, miss 1 dc, 1 tr into next dc, rep from * to end, turn.
Row 27: 1 ch (does NOT count as st), 1 dc into first tr, *1 dc into next ch sp, 1 dc into next tr, rep from * to end, working dc at end of last rep into 3rd of 4 ch at beg of previous row, turn. 133 sts.
Row 28: 1 ch (does NOT count as st), 1 dc into each dc to end, turn.
Rows 29 and 30: As row 28.
Row 31: 5 ch (counts as first ttr), miss dc at base of 5 ch, 1 ttr into each of next 2 dc, *3 ch, miss 3 dc, 1 ttr into each of next 3 dc, rep from * to last 4 sts, 3 ch, miss 3 dc, 1 ttr into last dc, turn.
Row 32: 1 ch (does NOT count as st), 1 dc into first ttr, *3 dc into next ch sp, 1 dc into each of next 3 ttr, rep from * to end, working dc at end of last rep into top of 5 ch at beg of previous row, turn.
Rows 33 to 35: As row 28.
Row 36: 3 ch (counts as first tr), miss first 2 dc, 1 tr into next dc, *1 ch, miss 1 dc, 1 tr into next dc, rep from * to end, turn.
Row 37: 1 ch (does NOT count as st), 1 dc into tr at base of 1 ch, *1 dc into next ch sp, 1 dc into next tr, rep from * to last 3 sts, 1 dc into next ch sp, dc2tog over last 2 sts (this is 1 tr and 3 ch at beg of previous row), turn.
Row 38: 1 ch (does NOT count as st), dc2tog over first 2 sts, 1 dc into each dc to end, turn.
Row 39: 5 ch (counts as first ttr), miss dc at base of 5 ch, 1 ttr into each of next 2 dc, *3 ch, miss 3 dc, 1 ttr into each of next 3 dc, rep from * to last 7 sts, 2 ch, miss 3 dc, ttr4tog over last 4 sts, turn.
Row 40: 1 ch (does NOT count as st), miss ttr4tog, 2 dc into first ch sp, *1 dc into each of next 3 ttr**, 3 dc into next ch sp, rep from * to end, ending last rep at ** with a dc into top of 5 ch at beg of previous row, turn.
Row 41: 1 ch (does NOT count as st), 1 dc into each dc to last 2 dc, dc2tog over last 2 dc, turn.
Row 42: 3 ch (does NOT count as st), miss st at base of 3 ch, 1 tr into next dc, miss 1 dc, 1 tr into next dc, *1 ch, miss 1 dc, 1 tr into next dc, rep from * to end, turn.
Row 43: 1 ch (does NOT count as st), 1 dc into first tr, *1 dc into next ch sp, 1 dc into next tr, rep from * to last 3 sts, 1 dc into next ch sp, dc2tog over last 2 tr, turn.
Row 44: As row 38. 120 sts.
Row 45: As row 41.
Row 46: As row 38. 118 sts.
Row 47: Ss across and into 6th st, 1 ch (does NOT count as st), 1 dc into same place as last ss, 1 dc into each of next 3 dc, 3 ch, miss 3 dc, 1 tr into each of next 3 dc, 3 ch, miss 3 dc, 1 dtr into each of next 2 dc, 1 ttr into next dc, (3 ch, miss 3 dc, 1 ttr into each of next 3 dc) 15 times, 2 ch, miss 3 dc, ttr4tog over last 4 sts, turn.
Row 48: 1 ch (does NOT count as st), miss ttr4tog, 2 dc into first ch sp, (1 dc into each of next 3 ttr, 3 dc into next ch sp) 14 times, 1 dc into each of next 2 ttr, turn, leaving rem 25 sts unworked.
Row 49: Ss across and into 6th st, 1 ch (does NOT count as st), 1 dc into same place as last ss, 1 dc into each dc to last 2 dc, dc2tog over last 2 dc, turn.

Row 50: 1 ch (does NOT count as st), dc2tog over first 2 sts, 1 dc into each of next 75 dc, turn, leaving rem 35 sts unworked.
Row 51: As row 49.
Row 52: 3 ch (does NOT count as st), miss st at base of 3 ch, 1 tr into next dc, miss 1 dc, 1 tr into next dc, (1 ch, miss 1 dc, 1 tr into next dc) 28 times, (1 ch, miss 1 dc, 1 dc into next dc) twice, 1 dc into next dc, turn, leaving rem 45 sts unworked.
Row 53: Ss across and into 11th st, 1 ch (does NOT count as st), 1 dc into ch sp at base of 1 ch, ★1 dc into next tr, 1 dc into next ch sp, rep from ★ to last 2 sts, dc2tog over last 2 tr, turn.
Row 54: 1 ch (does NOT count as st), dc2tog over first 2 sts, 1 dc into each of next 45 dc, turn, leaving rem 60 sts unworked.
Row 55: Ss across and into 6th st, 1 ch (does NOT count as st), 1 dc into dc at base of 1 ch, 1 dc into each of next 3 dc, 3 ch, miss 3 dc, 1 tr into each of next 2 dc, 1 dtr into next dc, (3 ch, miss 3 dc, 1 ttr into each of next 3 dc) 4 times, 2 ch, miss 3 dc, ttr4tog over last 4 sts, turn.
Row 56: 1 ch (does NOT count as st), miss ttr4tog, 2 dc into first ch sp, (1 dc into each of next 3 ttr, 3 dc into next ch sp) twice, 1 dc into each of next 3 ttr, 2 dc into next ch sp, turn, leaving rem 82 sts unworked.
Row 57: Ss across and into 5th st, 1 ch (does NOT count as st), 1 dc into same place as last ss, 1 dc into each of next 14 dc, turn.
Row 58: 1 ch (does NOT count as st), 1 dc into first dc, (1 ch, miss 1 dc, 1 dc into next dc) 5 times.
Fasten off.
Rejoin yarn at beg of row 58.
All sizes
Break off contrasts and cont using yarn A **only**.
Next row: 1 ch (does NOT count as st), 1 dc into each st to end, turn. 97 [99: 101: 101: 101] sts.
Next row: 1 ch (does NOT count as st), 1 dc into each dc to end, turn.
Rep last row once more.
Fasten off.

MAKING UP
Press as described on the information page.
Join right shoulder seam using back stitch, or mattress stitch if preferred.
Neckband
With RS facing, using 2¾mm (US 2) needles and yarn D, pick up and knit 44 [44: 48: 48: 50] sts down left side of neck, 29 [29: 31: 31: 33] sts from front, 44 [44: 48: 48: 50] sts up right side of neck, then 64 [64: 66: 66: 68] sts from back. 181 [181: 193: 193: 201] sts.
Beg with row 2, work in rib as given for back for 3 rows, ending with RS facing for next row.
Cast off in rib.
See information page for finishing instructions, setting in sleeves using the set-in method.
Cuff edgings (both alike)
With RS facing, using 3.00mm (US C2) crochet hook and yarn A, attach yarn at base of sleeve seam, 1 ch (does NOT count as st), work 1 round of dc evenly around cuff edge of sleeve, ending with ss to first dc, turn.
Next round: 1 ch (does NOT count as st), 1 dc into each dc to end, ss to first dc, turn.
Rep last round twice more.
Fasten off.

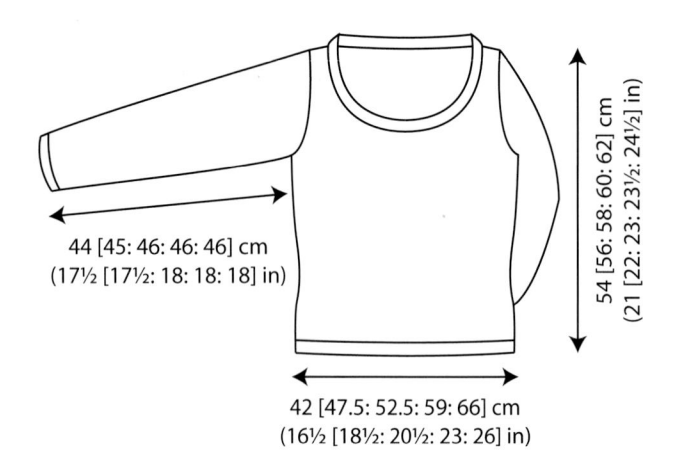

44 [45: 46: 46: 46] cm
(17½ [17½: 18: 18: 18] in)

54 [56: 58: 60: 62] cm
(21 [22: 23: 23½: 24½] in)

42 [47.5: 52.5: 59: 66] cm
(16½ [18½: 20½: 23: 26] in)

Pinot ★★

By Martin Storey

SIZES

S	M	L	XL	XXL	
To fit bust					
81-86	91-97	102-107	112-117	122-127	cm
32-34	36-38	40-42	44-46	48-50	in

YARN

Kidsilk Haze and Anchor Artiste Metallic

A Kidsilk Haze Steel 664

| 4 | 5 | 5 | 6 | 7 | x 25gm |

B Metallic Silver 301

| 1 | 1 | 1 | 2 | 2 | x 25gm |

NEEDLES

1 pair 2¾mm (no 12) (US 2) needles
1 pair 3¼mm (no 10) (US 3) needles

TENSION

25 sts and 34 rows to 10 cm measured over st st using 3¼mm (US 3) needles and yarn A.

BACK

Using 2¾mm (US 2) needles and yarn A cast on 110 [122: 138: 154: 170] sts.
Row 1 (RS): K2, *P2, K2, rep from * to end.
Row 2: P2, *K2, P2, rep from * to end.
These 2 rows form rib.
Cont in rib, dec 1 st at each end of 13th and 3 foll 6th rows. 102 [114: 130: 146: 162] sts.
Work a further 3 rows, inc [inc: inc: dec: inc] 1 st at end of last row and ending with RS facing for next row. 103 [115: 131: 145: 163] sts.
Change to 3¼mm (US 3) needles.
Beg with a K row, now work in st st, shaping side seams by inc 1 st at each end of 11th and 5 foll 12th rows. 115 [127: 143: 157: 175] sts.
Cont straight until back meas 33 [34: 35: 36: 37] cm, ending with RS facing for next row.
Shape armholes
Cast off 6 [7: 8: 9: 10] sts at beg of next 2 rows.
103 [113: 127: 139: 155] sts.
Dec 1 st at each end of next 5 [7: 9: 9: 11] rows, then on foll 4 [5: 6: 8: 10] alt rows, then on foll 4th row. 83 [87: 95: 103: 111] sts.
Cont straight until armhole meas 20 [21: 22: 23: 24] cm, ending with RS facing for next row.
Shape shoulders and back neck
Cast off 7 [8: 9: 10: 11] sts at beg of next 2 rows. 69 [71: 77: 83: 89] sts.
Next row (RS): Cast off 7 [8: 9: 10: 11] sts, K until there are 12 [12: 13: 15: 16] sts on right needle and turn, leaving rem sts on a holder.
Work each side of neck separately.
Cast off 4 sts at beg of next row.
Cast off rem 8 [8: 9: 11: 12] sts.
With RS facing, rejoin yarn to rem sts, cast off centre 31 [31: 33: 33: 35] sts, K to end.
Complete to match first side, reversing shapings.

FRONT

Work as given for back until 26 [26: 28: 28: 30] rows less have been worked than on back to beg of shoulder shaping, ending with RS facing for next row.
Shape front neck
Next row (RS): K35 [37: 41: 45: 49] and turn, leaving rem sts on a holder.
Work each side of neck separately.
Dec 1 st at neck edge of next 8 rows, then on foll 3 [3: 4: 4: 5] alt rows, then on 2 foll 4th rows. 22 [24: 27: 31: 34] sts.
Work 3 rows, ending with RS facing for next row.
Shape shoulder
Cast off 7 [8: 9: 10: 11] sts at beg of next and foll alt row.
Work 1 row.
Cast off rem 8 [8: 9: 11: 12] sts.
With RS facing, rejoin yarn to rem sts, cast off centre 13 sts, K to end.
Complete to match first side, reversing shapings.

SLEEVES

Upper frill
Using 3¼mm (US 3) needles and yarn B cast on 304 [320: 336: 352: 368] sts.

**Break off yarn B and join in yarn A.

Row 1 (RS): *K2, lift 2nd st on right needle over first st and off right needle, rep from * to end. 152 [160: 168: 176: 184] sts.

Row 2: *P2tog, rep from * to end. 76 [80: 84: 88: 92] sts.***

Beg with a K row, work in st st for 4 rows, ending with RS facing for next row.

Break yarn and leave sts on a holder.**

Middle frill
Using 3¼mm (US 3) needles and yarn B cast on 280 [296: 312: 328: 344] sts.

Work as given for upper frill from ** to **, noting that there will be 70 [74: 78: 82: 86] sts after row 2.

Lower frill and main sleeve
Using 3¼mm (US 3) needles and yarn B cast on 264 [280: 296: 312: 328] sts.

Work as given for upper frill from ** to ***. 66 [70: 74: 78: 82] sts.

Beg with a K row, work in st st, inc 1 st at each end of 8th and foll alt row, ending with RS facing for next row. 70 [74: 78: 82: 86] sts.

Attach middle frill
Next row (RS): Holding **WS** of middle frill against RS of sts on needle, K tog first st of middle frill with first st on needles, *K tog next st of middle frill with next st on needles, rep from * to end. 70 [74:78: 82: 86] sts.

Beg with a P row, work in st st, inc 1 st at each end of next and foll 2 alt rows and ending with RS facing for next row. 76 [80: 84: 88: 92] sts.

Attach upper frill
Next row (RS): Holding **WS** of upper frill against RS of sts on needle, K tog first st of upper frill with first st on needles, *K tog next st of upper frill with next st on needles, rep from * to end. 76 [80: 84: 88: 92] sts.

Beg with a P row, work in st st, inc 1 st at each end of next and foll 6 alt rows. 90 [94: 98: 102: 106] sts.

Work 2 rows, ending with RS facing for next row.

Shape top
Cast off 6 [7: 8: 9: 10] sts at beg of next 2 rows. 78 [80: 82: 84: 86] sts.

Dec 1 st at each end of next 5 rows, then on every foll alt row until 42 sts rem, then on foll 5 rows, ending with RS facing for next row. 32 sts.

Cast off 4 sts at beg of next 4 rows.

Cast off rem 16 sts.

COLLAR
Upper frill
Using 3¼mm (US 3) needles and yarn B cast on 476 [476: 508: 508: 532] sts.

Break off yarn B and join in yarn A.

Row 1 (RS): *K2, lift 2nd st on right needle over first st and off right needle, rep from * to end. 238 [238: 254: 254: 266] sts.

Row 2: *P2tog, rep from * to end. 119 [119: 127: 127: 133] sts.

Beg with a K row, work in st st for 4 rows, ending with RS facing for next row.

Break yarn and leave sts on a holder.

Middle frill
Work as given for upper frill.

Lower frill and main collar
Work as given for upper frill until row 2 has been completed.

Beg with a K row, work in st st for 10 rows, ending with RS facing for next row.

Attach middle frill
Next row (RS): Holding **WS** of middle frill against RS of sts on needle, K tog first st of middle frill with first st on needles, *K tog next st of middle frill with next st on needles, rep from * to end.

Beg with a P row, work in st st for 5 rows, ending with RS facing for next row.

Attach upper frill
Next row (RS): Holding **WS** of upper frill against RS of sts on needle, K tog first st of upper frill with first st on needles, *K tog next st of upper frill with next st on needles, rep from * to end.

Beg with a P row, work in st st for 25 rows, ending with RS facing for next row.

Next row (RS): K1, *P1, K1, rep from * to end.

Next row: P1, *K1, P1, rep from * to end.

These 2 rows form rib.

Work in rib for a further 4 rows, ending with RS facing for next row.

Cast off in rib.

MAKING UP
Press as described on the information page.

Join both shoulder seams using back stitch, or mattress stitch if preferred. Join row-end edges of collar to form a loop, reversing seam for rib section. Positioning collar seam at centre back neck and using photograph as a guide, sew ribbed edge of collar to neck edge.

See information page for finishing instructions, setting in sleeves using the set-in method.

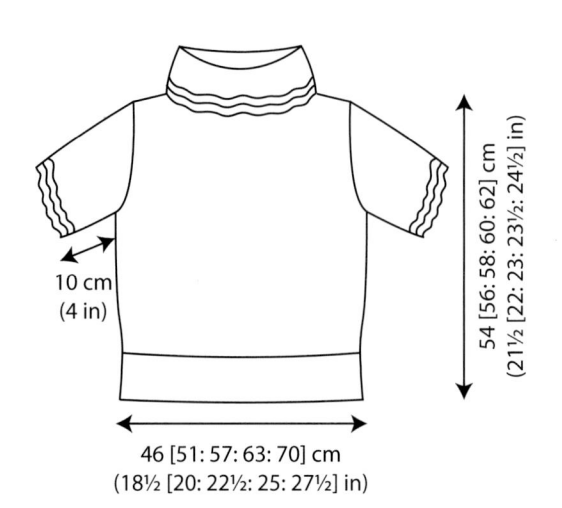

10 cm (4 in)

54 [56: 58: 60: 62] cm (21½ [22: 23: 23½: 24½] in)

46 [51: 57: 63: 70] cm (18½ [20: 22½: 25: 27½] in)

Sauvignon ★★
By Martin Storey

Main Image Page 16

SIZES

S	M	L	XL	XXL	
To fit bust					
81-86	91-97	102-107	112-117	122-127	cm
32-34	36-38	40-42	44-46	48-50	in

YARN
Kidsilk Haze

| 7 | 9 | 9 | 10 | 11 | x 25gm |

(photographed in Anthracite 639)

NEEDLES
1 pair 2¾mm (no 12) (US 2) needles
1 pair 3¼mm (no 10) (US 3) needles

BEADS - approx 1680 [1730: 1800: 1850: 1970] small glass beads

TENSION
25 sts and 34 rows to 10 cm measured over st st, 24 sts and 37 rows to 10 cm measured over beaded lace patt, both using 3¼mm (US 3) needles.

SPECIAL ABBREVIATION
bead 1 = place a bead by taking yarn to RS of work and slipping bead up next to st just worked, slip next st purlwise from left needle to right needle and bring yarn back to WS of work, leaving bead sitting in front of slipped st on RS.

Beading note: Before starting to knit, thread beads onto yarn. To do this, thread a fine sewing needle (one that will easily pass through the beads) with sewing thread. Knot ends of thread and then pass end of yarn through this loop. Thread a bead onto sewing thread and then gently slide it along and onto knitting yarn. Continue in this way until required number of beads are on yarn. Do not place beads on edge sts of rows as this will interfere with seaming.

BACK
Using 2¾mm (US 2) needles cast on 103 [115: 131: 145: 163] sts.
Row 1 (RS): K1, ★P1, K1, rep from ★ to end.
Row 2: P1, ★K1, P1, rep from ★ to end.
These 2 rows form rib.
Cont in rib for a further 16 rows, ending with RS facing for next row.
Change to 3¼mm (US 3) needles.
Beg with a K row, now work in st st, shaping side seams by inc 1 st at each end of 9th and 5 foll 12th rows. 115 [127: 143: 157: 175] sts.
Cont straight until back meas 32 [33: 34: 35: 36] cm, ending with RS facing for next row.
Shape armholes
Cast off 6 [7: 8: 9: 10] sts at beg of next 2 rows.
103 [113: 127: 139: 155] sts.★★
Dec 1 st at each end of next 5 [7: 9: 9: 11] rows, then on foll 4 [5: 6: 8: 10] alt rows, then on foll 4th row. 83 [87: 95: 103: 111] sts.
Cont straight until armhole meas 20 [21: 22: 23: 24] cm, ending with RS facing for next row.
Shape shoulders and back neck
Cast off 5 [6: 7: 8: 9] sts at beg of next 2 rows. 73 [75: 81: 87: 93] sts.
Next row (RS): Cast off 5 [6: 7: 8: 9] sts, K until there are 10 [10: 11: 13: 14] sts on right needle and turn, leaving rem sts on a holder.
Work each side of neck separately.
Cast off 4 sts at beg of next row.
Cast off rem 6 [6: 7: 9: 10] sts.
With RS facing, rejoin yarn to rem sts, cast off centre 43 [43: 45: 45: 47] sts, K to end.
Complete to match first side, reversing shapings.

FRONT
Work as given for back to ★★.
Dec 1 st at each end of next 5 [7: 9: 9: 11] rows, then on foll 1 [2: 1: 3: 2] alt rows. 91 [95: 107: 115: 129] sts.
Work 1 row, ending with RS facing for next row.
Shape front neck
Next row (RS): K2tog, K34 [36: 41: 45: 51] and turn, leaving rem sts on a holder.
Work each side of neck separately.
Dec 1 st at neck edge of next 8 rows, then on foll 4 alt rows, then on 2 foll 4th rows, then on foll 6th row, then on foll 8th row **and at same time** dec 1 st at armhole edge on 2nd and foll 2 [2: 4: 4: 7] alt rows.

16 [18: 21: 25: 28] sts.
Cont straight until front matches back to beg of shoulder shaping, ending with RS facing for next row.
Shape shoulder
Cast off 5 [6: 7: 8: 9] sts at beg of next and foll alt row.
Work 1 row.
Cast off rem 6 [6: 7: 9: 10] sts.
With RS facing, rejoin yarn to rem sts, cast off centre 19 [19: 21: 21: 23] sts, K to last 2 sts, K2tog.
Complete to match first side, reversing shapings.

SLEEVES
Using 2¾mm (US 2) needles cast on 57 [63: 63: 69: 75] sts.
Work in rib as given for back for 2 rows, ending with RS facing for next row.
Change to 3¼mm (US 3) needles.
Now work in beaded lace patt as folls:
Row 1 (RS): K2, *K2tog, yfwd, K1, yfwd, sl 1, K1, psso, K1, rep from * to last st, K1.
Row 2: Purl.
Row 3: K1, K2tog, yfwd, *K3, yfwd, sl 1, K2tog, psso, yfwd, rep from * to last 6 sts, K3, yfwd, sl 1, K1, psso, K1.
Row 4: *P4, bead 1, P1, rep from * to last 3 sts, P3.
Row 5: Inc in first st, K1, *yfwd, sl 1, K1, psso, K1, K2tog, yfwd, K1, rep from * to last st, inc in last st. 59 [65: 65: 71: 77] sts.
Row 6: Purl.
Row 7: (Inc in first st) 0 [0: 1: 0: 0] times, K3 [3: 2: 3: 3], *K1, yfwd, sl 1, K2tog, psso, yfwd, K2, rep from * to last 2 sts, K2 [2: 1: 2: 2], (inc in last st) 0 [0: 1: 0: 0] times. 59 [65: 67: 71: 77] sts.
Row 8: P2 [2: 3: 2: 2], *bead 1, P5, rep from * to last 3 [3: 4: 3: 3] sts, bead 1, P2 [2: 3: 2: 2].
These 8 rows form beaded lace patt and beg sleeve shaping.
Cont in beaded lace patt, shaping sides by inc 1 st at each end of next and 10 [7: 10: 10: 7] foll 4th rows, then on 0 [2: 0: 0: 2] foll 6th rows, taking inc sts into patt. 81 [85: 89: 93: 97] sts.
Work 5 rows, ending with RS facing for next row. (Sleeve should meas approx 15 cm.)
Shape top
Keeping patt correct, cast off 6 [7: 8: 9: 10] sts at beg of next 2 rows.

69 [71: 73: 75: 77] sts.
Dec 1 st at each end of next 3 rows, then on foll 3 alt rows, then on 3 foll 4th rows. 51 [53: 55: 57: 59] sts.
Work 1 row.
Dec 1 st at each end of next and every foll alt row until 35 sts rem, then on foll 9 rows, ending with RS facing for next row.
Cast off rem 17 sts.

COLLAR
Using 3¼mm (US 3) needles cast on 237 [237: 243: 243: 255] sts.
Work in rib as given for back for 2 rows, ending with RS facing for next row.
Now work in beaded lace patt as folls:
Row 1 (RS): K2, *K2tog, yfwd, K1, yfwd, sl 1, K1, psso, K1, rep from * to last st, K1.
Row 2: Purl.
Row 3: K1, K2tog, yfwd, *K3, yfwd, sl 1, K2tog, psso, yfwd, rep from * to last 6 sts, K3, yfwd, sl 1, K1, psso, K1.
Row 4: *P4, bead 1, P1, rep from * to last 3 sts, P3.
Row 5: K2, *yfwd, sl 1, K1, psso, K1, K2tog, yfwd, K1, rep from * to last st, K1.
Row 6: Purl.
Row 7: K2, *K1, yfwd, sl 1, K2tog, psso, yfwd, K2, rep from * to last st, K1.
Row 8: P1, *bead 1, P5, rep from * to last 2 sts, bead 1, P1.
These 8 rows form beaded lace patt.
Cont in beaded lace patt, dec 1 st at each end of next and every foll 4th row until 185 [185: 191: 191: 203] sts rem.
Work 3 rows, ending with RS facing for next row.
Cast off.

MAKING UP
Press as described on the information page.
Join both shoulder seams using back stitch, or mattress stitch if preferred.
Join row-end edges of collar to form a loop. Positioning collar seam at centre back neck, sew cast-off edge of collar to neck edge, easing in slight fullness.
See information page for finishing instructions, setting in sleeves using the set-in method.

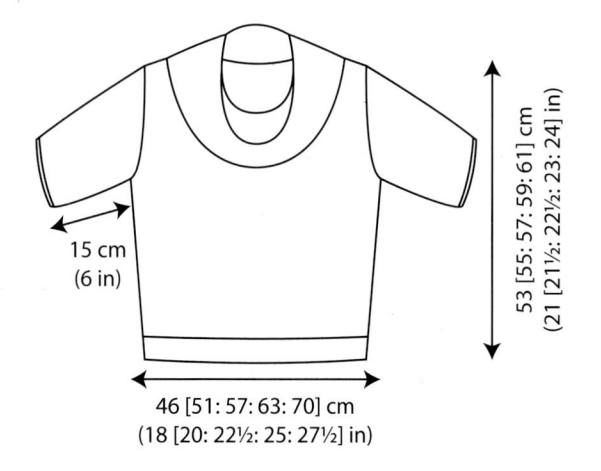

15 cm
(6 in)

46 [51: 57: 63: 70] cm
(18 [20: 22½: 25: 27½] in)

53 [55: 57: 59: 61] cm
(21 [21½: 22½: 23: 24] in)

Semillon ★★

By Martin Storey

Main Image Page 20

SIZES

S	M	L	XL	XXL	
To fit bust					
81-86	91-97	102-107	112-117	122-127	cm
32-34	36-38	40-42	44-46	48-50	in

YARN

Kidsilk Haze

4	4	5	5	6	x 25gm

(photographed in Blackcurrant 641)

NEEDLES

1 pair 2¾mm (no 12) (US 2) needles
1 pair 3¼mm (no 10) (US 3) needles

BEADS - approx 180 [190: 210: 230: 250] small glass beads

TENSION

25 sts and 34 rows to 10 cm measured over st st using 3¼mm (US 3) needles.

SPECIAL ABBREVIATION

bead 1 = place a bead by taking yarn to RS of work and slipping bead up next to st just worked, slip next st purlwise from left needle to right needle and take yarn back to WS of work, leaving bead sitting in front of slipped st on RS.

Beading note: Before starting to knit, thread beads onto yarn. To do this, thread a fine sewing needle (one that will easily pass through the beads) with sewing thread. Knot ends of thread and then pass end of yarn through this loop. Thread a bead onto sewing thread and then gently slide it along and onto knitting yarn. Continue in this way until required number of beads are on yarn. Do not place beads on edge sts of rows as this will interfere with seaming.

BACK

Using 2¾mm (US 2) needles cast on 123 [131: 147: 163: 179] sts.
Row 1 (RS): K1, *P1, K1, rep from * to end.
Row 2: P1, *K1, P1, rep from * to end.
These 2 rows form rib.
Change to 3¼mm (US 3) needles.
Now work in border patt as folls:
Row 1 (RS): Knit.
Row 2: Purl.
Row 3: K1, *yfwd, K2tog, rep from * to end.
Row 4: Purl.
Rows 5 and 6: As rows 1 and 2.
Row 7: K2, *K1, K2tog, yfwd, K1, yfwd, sl 1, K1, psso, K2, rep from * to last st, K1.
Row 8: P1, *P1, P2tog tbl, yrn, P3, yrn, P2tog, rep from * to last 2 sts, P2.
Row 9: K1, K2tog, yfwd, *K2, bead 1, K2, yfwd, sl 1, K2tog, psso, yfwd, rep from * to last 8 sts, K2, bead 1, K2, yfwd, sl 1, K1, psso, K1.
Row 10: P1, *P1, yrn, P2tog, P3, P2tog tbl, yrn, rep from * to last 2 sts, P2.
Row 11: K2, *K1, yfwd, sl 1, K1, psso, K1, K2tog, yfwd, K2, rep from * to last st, K1.
Row 12: P1, *P3, yrn, P3tog, yrn, P2, rep from * to last 2 sts, P2.
These 12 rows form border patt.
Keeping patt correct, cont in border patt, dec 1 st at each end of 3rd and 3 [3: 5: 5: 3] foll 6th [8th: 6th: 6th: 8th] rows, then on 3 [1: -: -: 1] foll 4th [6th: -: -: 6th] rows. 109 [121: 135: 151: 169] sts.
Work 7 rows, ending after patt row 4 and with RS facing for next row.
Beg with a K row, cont in st st, inc 1 st at each end of 17th and 5 foll 8th rows. 121 [133: 147: 163: 181] sts.
Cont straight until back meas 37 [38: 39: 40: 41] cm, ending with RS facing for next row.

Shape armholes
Cast off 4 sts at beg of next 2 rows. 113 [125: 139: 155: 173] sts.
Dec 1 st at each end of next and foll 7 alt rows.
97 [109: 123: 139: 157] sts.
Cont straight until armhole meas 18 [19: 20: 21: 22] cm, ending with RS facing for next row.

Shape back neck
Next row (RS): K25 [31: 37: 45: 53] and turn, leaving rem sts on a holder.

Work each side of neck separately.

Dec 1 st at neck edge of next 5 rows, ending with RS facing for next row. 20 [26: 32: 40: 48] sts.

Shape shoulder

Cast off 6 [8: 10: 12: 15] sts at beg of next and foll alt row **and at same time** dec 1 st at neck edge of next 3 rows.

Work 1 row.

Cast off rem 5 [7: 9: 13: 15] sts.

With RS facing, rejoin yarn to rem sts, cast off centre 47 [47: 49: 49: 51] sts, K to end.

Complete to match first side, reversing shapings.

FRONT

Work as given for back until 30 [30: 32: 32: 34] rows less have been worked than on back to beg of shoulder shaping, ending with RS facing for next row.

Shape front neck

Next row (RS): K33 [39: 46: 54: 63] and turn, leaving rem sts on a holder.

Work each side of neck separately.

Dec 1 st at neck edge of next 10 rows, then on foll 4 [4: 5: 5: 6] alt rows, then on 2 foll 4th rows. 17 [23: 29: 37: 45] sts.

Work 3 rows, ending with RS facing for next row.

Shape shoulder

Cast off 6 [8: 10: 12: 15] sts at beg of next and foll alt row.

Work 1 row.

Cast off rem 5 [7: 9: 13: 15] sts.

With RS facing, rejoin yarn to rem sts, cast off centre 31 sts, K to end.

Complete to match first side, reversing shapings.

SLEEVES

Using 2¾mm (US 2) needles cast on 99 [105: 109: 115: 121] sts.

Work in rib as given for back for 2 rows, ending with RS facing for next row.

Change to 3¼mm (US 3) needles.

Now work in border patt as folls:

Row 1 (RS): Knit.

Row 2: Purl.

Row 3: K1, ★yfwd, K2tog, rep from ★ to end.

Row 4: Purl.

Rows 5 and 6: As rows 1 and 2.

Row 7: K2 [1: 3: 2: 1], ★K1, K2tog, yfwd, K1, yfwd, sl 1, K1, psso, K2, rep from ★ to last 1 [0: 2: 1: 0] sts, K1 [0: 2: 1: 0].

Row 8: P1 [0: 2: 1: 0], ★P1, P2tog tbl, yrn, P3, yrn, P2tog, rep from ★ to last 2 [1: 3: 2: 1] sts, P2 [1: 3: 2: 1].

Row 9: K1 [0: 2: 1: 0], K2tog, yfwd, ★K2, bead 1, K2, yfwd, sl 1, K2tog, psso, yfwd, rep from ★ to last 8 [7: 9: 8: 7] sts, K2, bead 1, K2, yfwd, sl 1, K1, psso, K1 [0: 2: 1: 0].

Row 10: P1 [0: 2: 1: 0], ★P1, yrn, P2tog, P3, P2tog tbl, yrn, rep from ★ to last 2 [1: 3: 2: 1] sts, P2 [1: 3: 2: 1].

Row 11: K2 [1: 3: 2: 1], ★K1, yfwd, sl 1, K1, psso, K1, K2tog, yfwd, K2, rep from ★ to last 1 [0: 2: 1: 0] sts, K1 [0: 2: 1: 0].

Row 12: P1 [0: 2: 1: 0], ★P3, yrn, P3tog, yrn, P2, rep from ★ to last 2 [1: 3: 2: 1] sts, P2 [1: 3: 2: 1].

These 12 rows form border patt.

Shape top

Keeping border patt correct, cast off 4 sts at beg of next 2 rows. 91 [97: 101: 107: 113] sts.

Dec 1 st at each end of next and foll 6 alt rows, then on foll row, ending with RS facing for next row.

Cast off rem 75 [81: 85: 91: 97] sts.

MAKING UP

Press as described on the information page.

Join right shoulder seam using back stitch, or mattress stitch if preferred.

Neckband

With RS facing and using 2¾mm (US 2) needles, pick up and knit 30 [30: 32: 32: 34] sts down left side of neck, 31 sts from front, 30 [30: 32: 32: 34] sts up right side of neck, then 68 [68: 70: 70: 72] sts from back. 159 [159: 165: 165: 171] sts.

Beg with row 2, work in rib as given for back for 5 rows, ending with RS facing for next row.

Cast off in rib.

See information page for finishing instructions, setting in sleeves using the shallow set-in method.

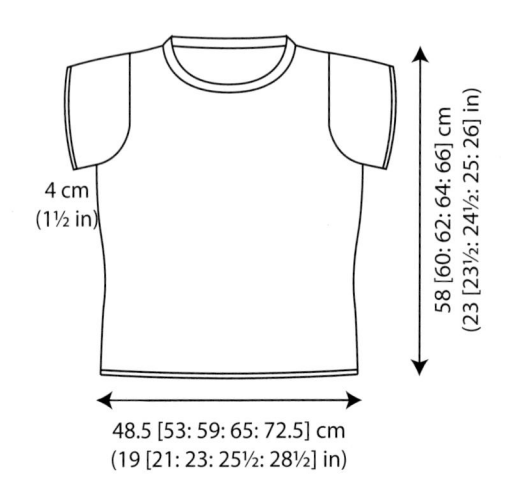

4 cm (1½ in)

48.5 [53: 59: 65: 72.5] cm (19 [21: 23: 25½: 28½] in)

58 [60: 62: 64: 66] cm (23 [23½: 24½: 25: 26] in)

Viognier ★★
By Lisa Richardson

Main Image Page 22

SIZES

S	M	L	XL	XXL	
To fit bust					
81-86	91-97	102-107	112-117	122-127	cm
32-34	36-38	40-42	44-46	48-50	in

YARN

Kidsilk Haze, Anchor Artiste Metallic and Fine Lace

A Kidsilk Haze Brick 649

3	3	3	3	4	x 25gm

B Metallic Pale Gold 302

1	1	2	2	2	x 25gm

C Kidsilk Haze Majestic 589

2	2	2	2	2	x 25gm

D Fine Lace Cameo 920

1	1	1	1	1	x 50gm

E Metallic Bronze 314

2	2	3	3	3	x 25gm

NEEDLES

1 pair 2¼mm (no 13) (US 1) needles
1 pair 3mm (no 11) (US 2/3) needles

TENSION

30 sts and 43 rows to 10 cm measured over striped st st using 3mm (US 2/3) needles.

STRIPE SEQUENCE

Rows 1 to 6: Using yarn A.
Rows 7 and 8: Using yarn B.
Rows 9 and 10: Using yarn C.
Rows 11 to 14: Using yarn D.
Rows 15 and 16: Using yarn E.
Rows 17 to 22: Using yarn C.
Rows 23 and 24: Using yarn A.
Rows 25 and 26: Using yarn E.
Rows 27 to 32: Using yarn D.
Rows 33 and 34: Using yarn B.
Rows 35 to 38: Using yarn A.
Rows 39 and 40: Using yarn E.
Rows 41 to 44: Using yarn C.
These 44 rows form stripe sequence and are repeated throughout.

BACK

Using 2¼mm (US 1) needles and yarn A cast on 129 [145: 159: 181: 201] sts.
Row 1 (RS): K1, ★P1, K1, rep from ★ to end.
Row 2: P1, ★K1, P1, rep from ★ to end.
These 2 rows form rib.
Work in rib for a further 34 rows, ending with RS facing for next row.
Change to 3mm (US 2/3) needles.
Beg with a K row and stripe row 1, now work in st st in stripe sequence (see above) throughout as folls:
Dec 1 st at each end of 3rd and 4 foll 4th rows.
119 [135: 149: 171: 191] sts.
Cont straight until back meas 19 [20: 21: 22: 23] cm, ending with RS facing for next row.★★
Inc 1 st at each end of next and 4 foll 12th rows.
129 [145: 159: 181: 201] sts.
Work 23 rows, ending with RS facing for next row. (Back should meas approx 36 [37: 38: 39: 40] cm.)

Shape armholes

Keeping stripes correct, cast off 5 [6: 7: 9: 11] sts at beg of next 2 rows.
119 [133: 145: 163: 179] sts.
Dec 1 st at each end of next 5 [7: 7: 9: 11] rows, then on foll 4 [6: 7: 10: 11] alt rows, then on foll 4th row. 99 [105: 115: 123: 133] sts.
Cont straight until armhole meas 18 [19: 20: 21: 22] cm, ending with RS facing for next row.

Shape back neck

Next row (RS): K25 [28: 31: 35: 39] and turn, leaving rem sts on a holder.
Work each side of neck separately.
Dec 1 st at neck edge of next 3 rows, ending with RS facing for next row. 22 [25: 28: 32: 36] sts.

Shape shoulder

Dec 1 st at neck edge of next 4 rows, ending with RS facing for next row, **and at same time** cast off 6 [7: 8: 9: 11] sts at beg of next and

foll alt row.
Cast off rem 6 [7: 8: 10: 10] sts.
With RS facing, rejoin appropriate yarn to rem sts, cast off centre 49 [49: 53: 53: 55] sts, K to end.
Complete to match first side, reversing shapings.

FRONT
Work as given for back to **.
Inc 1 st at each end of next and foll 12th row.
123 [139: 153: 175: 195] sts.
Work 3 rows, ending with RS facing for next row.
Divide for front neck
Next row (RS): K61 [69: 76: 87: 97] and turn, leaving rem sts on a holder.
Work each side of neck separately.
Dec 1 st at neck edge of 2nd and foll 14 [12: 14: 12: 12] alt rows, then on 6 [7: 6: 7: 7] foll 4th rows **and at same time** inc 1 st at side seam edge of 8th and 2 foll 12th rows. 43 [52: 58: 70: 80] sts.
Work 1 row, ending with RS facing for next row.
Shape armhole
Keeping stripes correct, cast off 5 [6: 7: 9: 11] sts at beg of next row. 38 [46: 51: 61: 69] sts.
Work 1 row.
Dec 1 st at armhole edge of next 5 [7: 7: 9: 11] rows, then on foll 4 [6: 7: 10: 11] alt rows, then on foll 4th row **and at same time** dec 1 st at neck edge of next and 3 [4: 5: 6: 7] foll 4th rows, then on 0 [1: 0: 1: 1] foll 6th row. 24 [26: 30: 33: 37] sts.
Dec 1 st at neck edge **only** on 2nd [6th: 2nd: 4th: 4th] and 1 [0: 1: 0: 0] foll 6th row, then on 2 foll 8th rows, then on 2 foll 10th rows. 18 [21: 24: 28: 32] sts.
Cont straight until front matches back to beg of shoulder shaping, ending with RS facing for next row.
Shape shoulder
Cast off 6 [7: 8: 9: 11] sts at beg of next and foll alt row.
Work 1 row.
Cast off rem 6 [7: 8: 10: 10] sts.
With RS facing, slip centre st onto a holder, rejoin appropriate yarn to rem sts, K to end.
Complete to match first side, reversing shapings.

SLEEVES
Using 2¼mm (US 1) needles and yarn A cast on 57 [61: 63: 63: 67] sts.
Work in rib as given for back for 32 rows, ending with RS facing for next row.
Change to 3mm (US 2/3) needles.
Beg with a K row and stripe row 41 [41: 41: 3: 7], now work in st st in stripe sequence (see above) throughout as folls:
Inc 1 st at each end of 5th and every foll 6th row to 75 [75: 81: 105: 117] sts, then on every foll 8th [8th: 8th: 8th: -] row until there are 97 [101: 105: 111: -] sts.
Cont straight until sleeve meas approx 45 [46: 47: 47: 47] cm, ending after same stripe row as on back to beg of armhole shaping and with RS facing for next row.

Shape top
Keeping stripes correct, cast off 5 [6: 7: 9: 11] sts at beg of next 2 rows. 87 [89: 91: 93: 95] sts.
Dec 1 st at each end of next 5 rows, then on foll 4 alt rows, then on 3 foll 4th rows. 63 [65: 67: 69: 71] sts.
Work 1 row.
Dec 1 st at each end of next and every foll alt row until 47 sts rem, then on foll 7 rows, ending with RS facing for next row. 33 sts.
Cast off 3 sts at beg of next 4 rows.
Cast off rem 21 sts.

MAKING UP
Press as described on the information page.
Join right shoulder seam using back stitch, or mattress stitch if preferred.
Neckband
With RS facing, using 2¼mm (US 1) needles and yarn A, pick up and knit 138 [142: 146: 150: 154] sts down left side of neck, K st on holder at base of V and mark this st with a coloured thread, pick up and knit 138 [142: 146: 150: 154] sts up right side of neck, then 68 [68: 72: 72: 74] sts from back. 345 [353: 365: 373: 383] sts.
Beg with row 2, work in rib as given for back for 1 row.
Keeping rib correct as now set, cont as folls:
Row 2 (RS): Rib to within 1 st of marked st, slip 2 sts as though to K2tog (marked st is 2nd of these 2 sts), K1, pass 2 slipped sts over, rib to end.
Row 3: Rib to marked st, P marked st, rib to end.
Rep last 2 rows 3 times more. 337 [345: 357: 365: 375] sts.
Cast off in rib, still decreasing either side of marked st as before.
See information page for finishing instructions, setting in sleeves using the set-in method.

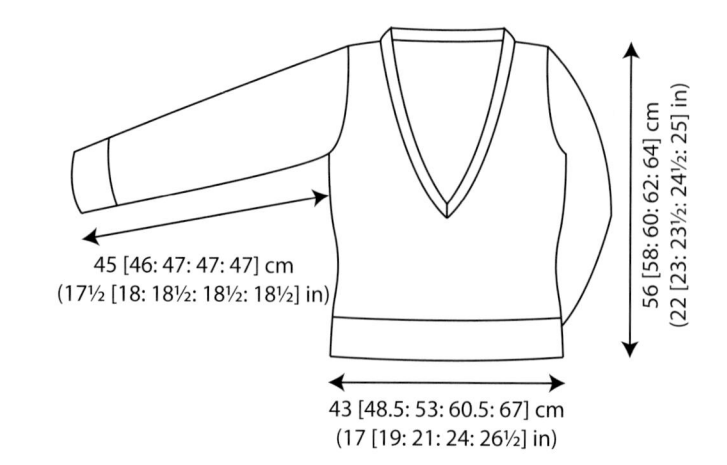

45 [46: 47: 47: 47] cm (17½ [18: 18½: 18½: 18½] in)

43 [48.5: 53: 60.5: 67] cm (17 [19: 21: 24: 26½] in)

56 [58: 60: 62: 64] cm (22 [23: 23½: 24½: 25] in)

Information

Tension
Obtaining the correct tension is perhaps the single factor which can make the difference between a successful garment and a disastrous one. It controls both the shape and size of an article, so any variation, however slight, can distort the finished garment. Different designers feature in our books and it is **their** tension, given at the **start** of each pattern, which you must match. We recommend that you knit a square in pattern and/or stocking stitch (depending on the pattern instructions) of perhaps 5 - 10 more stitches and 5 - 10 more rows than those given in the tension note. Mark out the central 10cm square with pins. If you have too many stitches to 10cm try again using thicker needles, if you have too few stitches to 10cm try again using finer needles. Once you have achieved the correct tension your garment will be knitted to the measurements indicated in the size diagram shown at the end of the pattern.

Sizing & Size Diagram Note
The instructions are given for the smallest size. Where they vary, work the figures in brackets for the larger sizes. **One set of figures refers to all sizes.** Included with most patterns in this magazine is a 'size diagram', of the finished garment and its dimensions. The measurement shown at the bottom of each **'size diagram'** shows the garment width 2.5cm below the armhole shaping. To help you choose the size of garment to knit please refer to the sizing guide on page 71.

Chart Note
Many of the patterns in the book are worked from charts. Each square on a chart represents a stitch and each line of squares a row of knitting. Each colour used is given a different letter and these are shown in the **materials** section, or in the **key** alongside the chart of each pattern. When working from the charts, read odd rows (K) from right to left and even rows (P) from left to right, unless otherwise stated. When working lace from a chart it is important to note that all but the largest size may have to alter the first and last few stitches in order not to lose or gain stitches over the row.

Working A Lace Pattern
When working a lace pattern it is important to remember that if you are unable to work both the increase and corresponding decrease and vica versa, the stitches should be worked in stocking stitch.

Finishing Instructions
After working for hours knitting a garment, it seems a great pity that many garments are spoiled because such little care is taken in the pressing and finishing process. Follow the text below for a truly professional-looking garment.

Pressing
Block out each piece of knitting and following the instructions on the ball band press the garment pieces, omitting the ribs. Tip: Take special care to press the edges, as this will make sewing up both easier and neater. If the ball band indicates that the fabric is not to be pressed, then covering the blocked out fabric with a damp white cotton cloth and leaving it to stand will have the desired effect. Darn in all ends neatly along the selvage edge or a colour join, as appropriate.

Stitching
When stitching the pieces together, remember to match areas of colour and texture very carefully where they meet. Use a seam stitch such as back stitch or mattress stitch for all main knitting seams and join all ribs and neckband with mattress stitch, unless otherwise stated.

Construction
Having completed the pattern instructions, join left shoulder and neckband seams as detailed above. Sew the top of the sleeve to the body of the garment using the method detailed in the pattern, referring to the appropriate guide:
Straight cast-off sleeves: Place centre of cast-off edge of sleeve to shoulder seam. Sew top of sleeve to body, using markers as guidelines where applicable.
Square set-in sleeves: Place centre of cast-off edge of sleeve to shoulder seam. Set sleeve head into armhole, the straight sides at top of sleeve to form a neat right-angle to cast-off sts at armhole on back and front.
Shallow set-in sleeves: Place centre of cast off edge of sleeve to shoulder seam. Match decreases at beg of armhole shaping to decreases at top of sleeve. Sew sleeve head into armhole, easing in shapings.
Set- in sleeves: Place centre of cast-off edge of sleeve to shoulder seam. Set in sleeve, easing sleeve head into armhole.

Join side and sleeve seams.
Slip stitch pocket edgings and linings into place.
Sew on buttons to correspond with buttonholes.
Ribbed welts and neckbands and any areas of garter stitch should not be pressed.

Buttons and Ribbons used in this Brochure are sourced from:
Bedecked Ltd,
5 Castle st.
Hay on Wye,
Herefordshire,
HR3 5DF

Tel: 01497 822769
Email: judith.lewis@bedecked.co.uk
Web: www.bedecked.co.uk

Beads used in this Brochure are Sourced From:
Dabeads
Tel: 0115 8551799
Email: beads@debbieabrahams.com

Rowan recommends MILWARD **Haberdashery Products**

Abbreviations

K	knit	M1	make one stitch by picking up horizontal loop before next stitch and knitting into back of it
P	purl		
st(s)	stitch(es)	M1P	make one stitch by picking up horizontal loop before next stitch and purling into back of it
inc	increas(e)(ing)		
dec	decreas(e)(ing)		
st st	stocking stitch (1 row K, 1 row P)	yfwd	yarn forward
g st	garter stitch (K every row)	yrn	yarn round needle
beg	begin(ning)	meas	measures
foll	following	0	no stitches, times or rows
rem	remain(ing)	-	no stitches, times or rows for that size
rev st st	reverse stocking stitch (1 row K, 1 row P)	yo	yarn over needle
rep	repeat	yfrn	yarn forward round needle
alt	alternate	wyib	with yarn at back
cont	continue	sl2togK	slip 2 stitches together knitways
patt	pattern		
tog	together		
mm	millimetres		
cm	centimetres		
in(s)	inch(es)		
RS	right side		
WS	wrong side		
sl 1	slip one stitch		
psso	pass slipped stitch over		
p2sso	pass 2 slipped stitches over		
tbl	through back of loop		

Crochet Terms

UK crochet terms and abbreviations have been used throughout. The list below gives the US equivalent where they vary.

Abbrev.	UK	US
dc	double crochet	single crochet
tr	treble	double crochet
dtr	double treble	treble
ttr	triple treble	double treble
qtr	quadruple treble	triple treble

Experience Rating

★

Easy, straight forward knitting

★ ★

Suitable for the average knitter

★ ★ ★

For the more experienced knitter

Sizing Guide

When you knit and wear a Rowan design we want you to look and feel fabulous. This all starts with the size and fit of the design you choose. To help you to achieve a great knitting experience we have looked at the sizing of our womens and menswear patterns. This has resulted in the introduction of our new sizing guide which includes the following exciting features:

Our sizing now conforms to standard clothing sizes. Therefore if you buy a standard size 12 in clothing, then our medium patterns will fit you perfectly.

The menswear designs are now available to knit in menswear sizes XSmall through to 2XL ie. 38" to 50" chest.

We have now added a UNISEX sizing guide. This is the SAME as the Mens standard sizing guide with an XXSmall size being added.

Dimensions in the charts below are body measurements, not garment dimensions, therefore please refer to the measuring guide to help you to determine which is the best size for you to knit.

STANDARD SIZING GUIDE FOR WOMEN

The sizing within this chart is also based on the larger size within the range, ie. M will be based on size 14

UK SIZE	S	M	L	XL	XXL	
DUAL SIZE	8/10	12/14	16/18	20/22	24/26	
To fit bust	32 – 34	36 – 38	40 – 42	44 – 46	48 – 50	inches
	81 – 86	91 – 97	102 – 107	112 – 117	122 – 127	cm
To fit waist	24 – 26	28 – 30	32 – 34	36 – 38	40 – 42	inches
	61 – 66	71 – 76	81 – 86	91 – 97	102 – 107	cm
To fit hips	34 – 36	38 – 40	42 – 44	46 – 48	50 – 52	inches

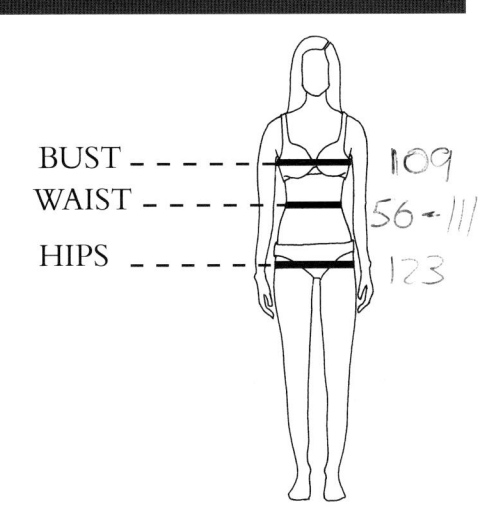

BUST — 109
WAIST — 56 – 111
HIPS — 123

SIZING & SIZE DIAGRAM NOTE

The instructions are given for the smallest size. Where they vary, work the figures in brackets for the larger sizes. One set of figures refers to all sizes. Included with most patterns in this magazine is a 'size diagram' - see image on the right, of the finished garment and its dimensions. The measurement shown at the bottom of each 'size diagram' shows the garment width 2.5cm below the armhole shaping. To help you choose the size of garment to knit please refer to the sizing guide. Generally in the majority of designs the welt width (at the cast on edge of the garment) is the same width as the chest. However, some designs are 'A-Line' in shape or flared edge and in these cases welt width will be wider than the chest width.

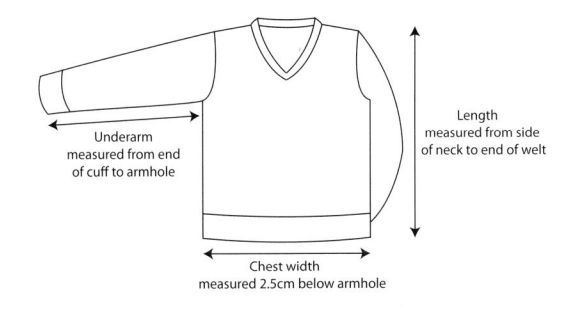

MEASURING GUIDE

For maximum comfort and to ensure the correct fit when choosing a size to knit, please follow the tips below when checking your size.
Measure yourself close to your body, over your underwear and don't pull the tape measure too tight!
Bust/chest – measure around the fullest part of the bust/chest and across the shoulder blades.
Waist – measure around the natural waistline, just above the hip bone.
Hips – measure around the fullest part of the bottom.
If you don't wish to measure yourself, note the size of a favourite jumper that you like the fit of. Our sizes are now comparable to the clothing sizes from the major high street retailers, so if your favourite jumper is a size Medium or size 12, then our casual size Medium and standard size 12 should be approximately the same fit.

To be extra sure, measure your favourite jumper and then compare these measurements with the Rowan size diagram given at the end of the individual instructions.
Finally, once you have decided which size is best for you, please ensure that you achieve the tension required for the design you wish to knit.
Remember if your tension is too loose, your garment will be bigger than the pattern size and you may use more yarn. If your tension is too tight, your garment could be smaller than the pattern size and you will have yarn left over.
Furthermore if your tension is incorrect, the handle of your fabric will be too stiff or floppy and will not fit properly. It really does make sense to check your tension before starting every project.

Stockist

AUSTRALIA: Australian Country Spinners, Pty Ltd, Level 7, 409 St. Kilda Road, Melbourne Vic 3004.
Tel: 03 9380 3888   Fax: 03 9820 0989   Email: customerservice@auspinners.com.au

AUSTRIA: Coats Harlander Ges.m.b.h, Autokaderstraße 29, BT2, 1.OG, 1210 Wien, Österreich
Tel: 00800 26 27 28 00   Fax: 00 49 7644 802-133   Email: coats.harlander@coats.com
Web: www.coatscrafts.at

BELGIUM: Coats N.V. c/o Coats GmbH Kaiserstr.1 79341 Kenzingen Germany
Tel: 0800 77892   Fax: 00 49 7644 802 133   Email: sales.coatsninove@coats.com
Web: www.coatscrafts.be

BULGARIA: Coats Bulgaria, 7 Magnaurska Shkola Str., BG-1784 Sofia, Bulgaria
Tel: (+359 2) 976 77 41   Fax: (+359 2) 976 77 20   Email: officebg@coats.com
Web: www.coatsbulgaria.bg

CANADA: Westminster Fibers, 10 Roybridge Gate, Suite 200 Vaughan, Ontario L4H 3M8
Tel: (800) 263-2354   Fax: 905 856 6184   Email: info@westminsterfibers.com

CHINA: Coats Shanghai Ltd, No 9 Building, Baosheng Road, Songjiang Industrial Zone, Shanghai.
Tel: +86 13816681825   Email: victor.li@coats.com,

CYPRUS: Coats Bulgaria, 7 Magnaurska Shkola Str., BG-1784 Sofia, Bulgaria
Tel: (+359 2) 976 77 41   Fax: (+359 2) 976 77 20   Email: officebg@coats.com
Web: www.coatscrafts.com.cy

ESTONIA: Coats Eesti AS, Ampri tee 9/4, 74010 Viimsi Harjumaa
Tel: +372 630 6250   Fax: +372 630 6260   Email: coats@coats.ee   Web: www.coatscrafts.co.ee

DENMARK: Coats Expotex AB, S-516 21 Dalsjöfors, Sweden
Tel: (45) 35 83 50 20   E-mail: kundeservice.dk@coats.com

FINLAND: Coats Opti Crafts Oy, Huhtimontie 6 04200 KERAVA
Tel: (358) 9 274871   Fax: (358) 9 2748 7330   Email: coatsopti.sales@coats.com   Web: www.coatscrafts.fi

FRANCE: Coats France, c/o Coats GmbH, Kaiserstr.1, 79341 Kenzingen, Germany
Tel: +32 (0) 0810 06 00 02   Fax: 0810 06 00 03   Email: artsdufil@coats.com   Web: www.coatscrafts.fr

GERMANY: Coats GmbH, Kaiserstrasse 1, 79341 Kenzingen, Germany
Tel: 0049 7644-802 222   Fax: 0049 7644-802 300   Email: kenzingen.vertrieb@coats.com Web: www.coatsgmbh.de

GREECE: Coats Bulgaria, 7 Magnaurska Shkola Str., BG-1784 Sofia, Bulgaria
Tel: (+359 2) 976 77 41   Fax: (+359 2) 976 77 20   Email: officebg@coats.com   Web: www.coatscrafts.gr

HOLLAND: Coats B.V. c/o Coats GmbH Kaiserstr.1 79341 Kenzingen, Germany
Tel: 0800 0226648   Fax: 00 49 7644 802 133   Email: sales.coatsninove@coats.com
Web: www.coatscrafts.be

HONG KONG: East Unity Company Ltd, Unit B2, 7/F., Block B, Kailey Industrial Centre, 12 Fung Yip Street, Chai Wan
Tel: (852)2869 7110   Email: eastunityco@yahoo.com.hk

ICELAND: Storkurinn, Laugavegi 59, 101 Reykjavik
Tel: (354) 551 8258   Email: storkurinn@simnet.is

ITALY: Coats Cucirini srl, Viale Sarca no 223, 20126 Milano
Tel: 0039 02636151   Fax: 00390266111701

KOREA: Coats Korea Co.,Ltd, 5F Telcom B/D, 935-40 Bangbae-Dong, Seocho-Gu, Seoul, Korea, 137-060
Tel: (82) 2 521 6262   Fax: (82) 2 521 5181   Email: rozenpark@coats.com

LATVIA: Coats Latvija SIA, Mukusalas str. 41 b, Riga LV-1004
Tel: +371 67625173   Fax: +371 67892758   Email: info.latvia@coats.com

LEBANON: y.knot, Saifi Village, Mkhalissiya Street 162, Beirut
Tel: (961) 1 992211   Fax: (961) 1 315553   Email: y.knot@cyberia.net.lb

LITHUANIA & RUSSIA: Coats Lietuva UAB, A. Juozapavicious str. 6/2, LT-09310 Vilnius
Tel: +370 527 30971   Fax: +370 527 2305   Email: info@coats.lt   Web: www.coatscrafts.lt

LUXEMBOURG: Coats N.V. c/o Coats GmbH Kaiserstr.1 79341 Kenzingen, Germany
Tel: 00 49 7644 802 222   Fax: 00 49 7644 802 133   Email: sales.coatsninove@coats.com
Web: www.coatscrafts.be

MALTA: John Gregory Ltd, 8 Ta'Xbiex Sea Front, Msida MSD 1512, Malta
Tel: +356 2133 0202   Fax: +356 2134 4745   Email: raygreg@onvol.net

MEXICO: Estambres Crochet SA de CV, PO Box SANTAMARIA, 64650 MONTERREY

NEW ZEALAND: ACS New Zealand, 1 March Place, Belfast, Christchurch
Tel: 64 3 323 6665   Fax: 64 3 323 6660

NORWAY: Coats Knappehuset AS, Hesthaugveien 15, 5119 Ulset
Tel: (47) 55 53 93 00   Fax: (47) 55 53 93 93   E-mail: post@coats.com

PORTUGAL: Coats & Clark Quinta de cravel, Apartado 4444, 4431-968 Vila Nova de Gaia
Tel: 00 351 223 770700

SINGAPORE: Golden Dragon Store, 101 Upper Cross Street #02-51, People's Park Centre, Singapore 058357
Tel: (65) 6 5358454   Fax: (65) 6 2216278   Email: gdscraft@hotmail.com

SOUTH AFRICA: Arthur Bales LTD, 62 4th Avenue, Linden 2195
Tel: (27) 11 888 2401   Fax: (27) 11 782 6137   Email: arthurb@new.co.za

SPAIN: Coats Fabra, Sant Adria 20, 08030 Barcelona
Tel: (34) 932908400   Fax: 932908409   Email: atencion.clientes@coats.com

SWEDEN: Coats Expotex AB, Stationsvägen 2, 516 21 Dalsjöfors
Tel: (46) 33 720 79 10   Fax: 46 33 720 79 40   E-mail: kundtjanst.dfs@coats.com

SWITZERLAND: Coats Stroppel AG, Stroppelstrasse 20, 5417 Untersiggenthal, Schweiz
Tel: 00800 2627 2800   Fax: 0049 7644 802 133   Email: coats.stroppel@coats.com
Web: coatscrafts.ch

TAIWAN: Cactus Quality Co Ltd, 7FL-2, No. 140, Sec.2 Roosevelt Rd, Taipei, 10084 Taiwan, R.O.C.
Tel: 00886-2-23656527   Fax: 886-2-23656503   Email: cqcl@ms17.hinet.net

THAILAND: Global Wide Trading, 10 Lad Prao Soi 88, Bangkok 10310
Tel: 00 662 933 9019   Fax: 00 662 933 9110   Email: global.wide@yahoo.com

U.S.A.: Westminster Fiber---Shelter Drive, Greer, South Carolina 29650
Tel: (800) 445-9276   Fax: 864-879-9432   Email: info@westminsterfibers.com

U.K.: Rowan, Green Lane Mill, Holmfirth, West Yorkshire, England HD9 2DX
Tel: +44 (0) 1484 681881   Fax: +44 (0) 1484 687920   Email: ccuk.sales@coats.com   Web: www.knitrowan.com

For stockists in all other countries please contact Rowan for details

Notes

Burgundy
Pattern page 32

Cabernet
Pattern page 35

Chablis
Pattern page 38

Champagne
Pattern page 41

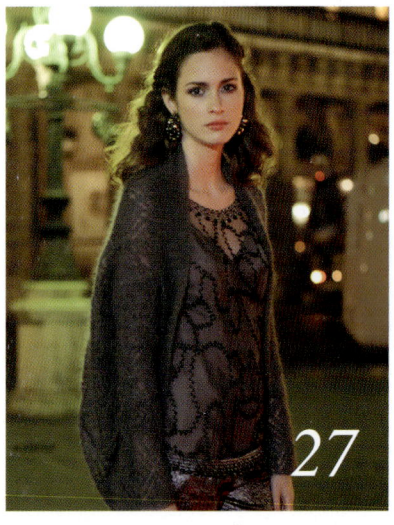

Chardonnay
Pattern page 43

Chenin
Pattern page 47

Merlot
Pattern page 51

Muscadet
Pattern page 53

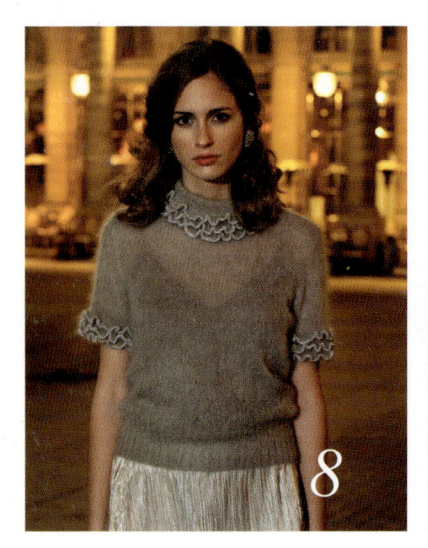

Pinot
Pattern page 61

Sauvignon
Pattern page 63

Semillon
Pattern page 65

Viognier
Pattern page 67